Personalization Engines

Advanced Recommender Systems for Digital Commerce

Author: Pegah Malekpour Alamdari

Editor: Gholamreza Zare

Table of Contents

Preface

In the rapidly evolving world of digital commerce, personalization has become the cornerstone of successful customer engagement. As consumers are bombarded with an overwhelming array of choices, the ability to deliver tailored recommendations can make the difference between a fleeting visit and a loyal customer. The journey towards building sophisticated recommender systems is both challenging and exhilarating, blending the art of understanding human preferences with the science of data and algorithms.

The inspiration for this book, "Personalization Engines: Advanced Recommender Systems for Digital Commerce," stems from my own experiences as a developer and researcher in the field of computer science. Throughout my career, I have witnessed firsthand the transformative power of personalization in driving business growth and enhancing user satisfaction. However, I have also seen the complexities and hurdles that developers face when embarking on the quest to build effective recommendation systems.

This book aims to demystify the intricacies of recommender systems, providing a comprehensive guide that bridges theory and practice. Whether you are a seasoned developer looking to refine your skills or a newcomer eager to dive into the world of personalized recommendations, this book offers valuable insights and practical knowledge to help you succeed.

We will explore the foundational concepts and various techniques that form the backbone of recommender systems, from collaborative filtering and content-based methods to advanced algorithms like deep learning and reinforcement learning. In addition, we will delve into the critical aspects of data preprocessing and evaluation metrics, ensuring that you have a holistic understanding of the entire development lifecycle.

One of the highlights of this book is the inclusion of real-world case studies that illustrate the practical applications and impact of recommender systems across different industries. These case studies provide not only inspiration but also valuable lessons and best practices that you can apply to your own projects.

As we embark on this journey together, I encourage you to approach each chapter with curiosity and an open mind. The field of recommender systems is dynamic and ever-changing, and continuous learning is key to staying ahead. I hope this book serves as a valuable resource, empowering you to build systems that deliver highly personalized and impactful product suggestions.

I would like to extend my gratitude to the many individuals who have contributed to this work. Your support, feedback, and encouragement have been instrumental in bringing this book to fruition.

Thank you for joining me on this exciting adventure. Let's dive in and explore the world of personalization engines together.

1. Introduction

In the contemporary digital era, the proliferation of information and the exponential growth of data have fundamentally transformed how individuals interact with technology. The sheer volume of content available on the internet, coupled with the diverse array of user preferences, necessitates sophisticated mechanisms to filter and personalize information. Recommender systems have emerged as critical tools in this landscape, playing a pivotal role in enhancing user experience by providing personalized content, products, and services. These systems leverage advanced algorithms and data analytics to predict user preferences and deliver tailored recommendations, thereby mitigating information overload and driving user engagement.

The origins of recommender systems can be traced back to the early 1990s, coinciding with the advent of the World Wide Web and the subsequent explosion of digital content. Initial recommendation approaches, primarily based on collaborative filtering and content-based filtering, laid the groundwork for more complex and nuanced systems. Collaborative filtering, which relies on the collective preferences of users, demonstrated significant potential in capturing the wisdom of the crowd to suggest items of interest. Content-based filtering, on the other hand, leveraged the attributes of items to align recommendations with individual user preferences. While these methods provided a solid foundation, their limitations, such as data sparsity and cold start problems, spurred the development of hybrid recommender systems that integrate multiple techniques to enhance accuracy and robustness.

The evolution of recommender systems has been marked by continuous innovation, driven by advances in machine learning and artificial intelligence. Deep learning, in particular, has revolutionized the field by enabling the extraction of high-dimensional feature representations and capturing complex patterns in user behavior and item characteristics. Techniques such as neural collaborative filtering, convolutional neural networks (CNNs), and recurrent neural networks (RNNs) have significantly improved the ability of recommender systems to model user-item interactions and provide personalized recommendations. For instance, neural collaborative filtering replaces traditional linear models with neural networks to capture non-linear relationships, resulting in more accurate and nuanced recommendations.

Attention mechanisms, introduced in the context of neural machine translation, have further enhanced the capability of recommender systems by allowing models to dynamically focus on the most relevant parts of the input data. This has proven particularly valuable in capturing temporal dependencies and contextual relevance, thereby improving the precision and personalization of recommendations. The self-attention mechanism, a cornerstone of transformer models, computes attention weights for each element in the input sequence relative to all other elements, enabling the capture of long-range dependencies and interactions. This has been instrumental in advancing the state-of-the-art in various applications, including personalized news feeds and content recommendations.

Reinforcement learning offers another promising avenue for the development of recommender systems, framing the recommendation process as a sequential decision-making problem. By optimizing for long-term user engagement and satisfaction, reinforcement learning algorithms adapt recommendations based on continuous feedback from user interactions. Techniques such as Q-learning and deep Q-networks (DQNs) have demonstrated their efficacy in balancing exploration and exploitation, providing a robust framework for adaptive and personalized recommendations. For example, in e-commerce and streaming services, reinforcement learning can dynamically adjust recommendations to align with evolving user preferences, thereby enhancing user retention and satisfaction.

The scalability and performance optimization of recommender systems are crucial to their practical deployment, especially given the increasing volume of data and the growing number of users. Distributed computing architectures, parallelization, efficient data structures, and online learning algorithms are essential strategies for managing large-scale data and ensuring real-time responsiveness. Techniques such as approximate nearest neighbor (ANN) search, model compression, and caching strategies reduce computational complexity and latency, enabling recommender systems to deliver timely and relevant recommendations. The implementation of these strategies in platforms like Amazon and Netflix underscores their importance in achieving high performance and scalability in real-world applications.

Despite the significant advancements, the implementation of recommender systems also presents challenges that necessitate ongoing research and innovation. Issues such as data sparsity, cold start problems, and the interpretability of complex models require careful consideration and sophisticated solutions. Ensuring fairness and mitigating biases in recommendations are also critical concerns, particularly as users increasingly demand transparency and ethical considerations in digital services. Addressing these challenges involves continuous evaluation and refinement of recommendation algorithms, supported by robust frameworks and user feedback.

In conclusion, recommender systems have become indispensable in the digital age, offering powerful tools for personalizing user experiences and enhancing engagement. The integration of advanced methodologies, including deep learning, attention mechanisms, reinforcement learning, and scalability optimization, has significantly elevated the capability of these systems to deliver accurate, relevant, and dynamic recommendations. As the field continues to evolve, the ongoing exploration and integration of these advanced techniques will remain essential to the development of next-generation recommender systems. By harnessing the potential of these technologies, developers can create sophisticated, responsive, and user-centric solutions that meet the diverse and ever-changing needs of users in an increasingly data-driven world.

2. Fundamentals of Recommender Systems

The realm of recommender systems is vast and multifaceted, encompassing a variety of techniques and methodologies aimed at predicting user preferences. Understanding the fundamentals is crucial for anyone aspiring to develop effective and sophisticated recommender systems. This chapter delves into the historical evolution, core types, and basic concepts that form the foundation of recommender systems, providing a comprehensive overview that sets the stage for the more advanced topics discussed in subsequent chapters.

2.1. Historical Evolution

The historical evolution of recommender systems traces back to the early stages of digital information proliferation, coinciding with the advent of the World Wide Web in the early 1990s. As the internet began to expand, the sheer volume of accessible content necessitated the development of mechanisms to filter and personalize information for users. Initial efforts in recommendation technologies primarily focused on collaborative filtering, a method that harnesses the collective preferences of users to generate personalized suggestions. The fundamental principle behind collaborative filtering is the assumption that users who have agreed in the past will continue to agree in the future, thereby leveraging the wisdom of the crowd to make accurate recommendations.

Collaborative filtering can be divided into two main categories: user-based and item-based collaborative filtering. User-based collaborative filtering identifies users with similar preferences to the target user and recommends items that these similar users have liked. Mathematically, this approach often involves calculating the similarity between users using measures such as the Pearson correlation coefficient or cosine similarity. For instance, the similarity $s(u, v)$ between users u and v can be calculated using cosine similarity as follows:

$$s(u, v) = \frac{\sum_{i \in I_{uv}} r_{ui} r_{vi}}{\sqrt{\sum_{i \in I_u} r_{ui}^2} \sqrt{\sum_{i \in I_v} r_{vi}^2}}$$

where r_{ui} and r_{vi} are the ratings given by users u and v to item i, and I_{uv} is the set of items rated by both users. Item-based collaborative filtering, on the other hand, focuses on identifying items that are similar to those the target user has interacted with, using similar similarity measures to compare items based on user ratings. This approach became particularly popular with platforms like Amazon, which utilized item-based collaborative filtering to recommend products based on similarities in user purchasing behavior.

Despite their initial success, collaborative filtering techniques encountered significant challenges, notably the cold start problem and data sparsity. The cold start problem arises when there is insufficient data about new users or items, making it difficult to generate accurate recommendations. Data sparsity, on the other hand, refers to the situation where user-item interaction data is sparse, leading to unreliable similarity computations. These limitations spurred the development of content-based filtering methods, which leverage the attributes of items to make recommendations. Content-based filtering involves constructing a profile for each user based on the features of items they have interacted with, and recommending items with similar features. For example, in a movie recommendation system, content-based filtering might consider attributes such as genre, director, and actors to recommend movies similar to those the user has previously enjoyed.

The turn of the millennium witnessed the emergence of hybrid recommender systems, which integrate multiple recommendation techniques to overcome the limitations of individual methods and enhance overall performance. Hybrid systems combine collaborative and content-based filtering in various ways, such as by incorporating weighted combinations of the two approaches, switching between methods based on context, or using one method to generate candidates that are refined by another. This integration allows for a more robust recommendation framework that can handle a wider range of scenarios and user preferences.

The evolution of recommender systems took a significant leap forward with the advent of machine learning and artificial intelligence. The application of matrix factorization techniques, such as Singular Value Decomposition (SVD) and Alternating Least Squares (ALS), revolutionized collaborative filtering by decomposing the user-item interaction matrix into latent factors that capture underlying patterns in the data. These techniques enabled the identification of implicit user preferences and item characteristics, improving the accuracy of recommendations. The Netflix Prize competition in 2006 brought matrix factorization to the forefront, as participants developed sophisticated models to predict user ratings with unprecedented accuracy, ultimately leading to substantial advancements in recommendation algorithms.

The subsequent rise of deep learning further transformed the landscape of recommender systems. Deep learning models, with their ability to capture complex, non-linear relationships in data, have significantly enhanced the capabilities of recommender systems. Neural collaborative filtering, for instance, employs neural networks to learn high-dimensional embeddings for users and items, allowing for more nuanced modeling of user-item interactions. Convolutional neural networks (CNNs) and recurrent neural networks (RNNs) have also been utilized to process unstructured data, such as images, text, and sequential interactions, thereby enriching the feature representations used for recommendations. For example, CNNs can analyze visual content to recommend images or products based on their visual similarity, while RNNs can model sequential user behavior to predict future interactions.

Attention mechanisms, initially developed for neural machine translation, have also found applications in recommender systems. By allowing models to dynamically focus on the most relevant parts of the input data, attention mechanisms enhance the ability to capture temporal dependencies and contextual relevance. The self-attention mechanism, which computes attention weights for each element in the input sequence relative to all other elements, has been particularly influential. This mechanism enables the modeling of long-range dependencies and interactions, improving the precision of recommendations in applications such as personalized news feeds and content suggestions.

Reinforcement learning represents another significant advancement in the field, offering a framework for optimizing long-term user engagement and satisfaction. By modeling the recommendation process as a sequential decision-making problem, reinforcement learning algorithms can adapt recommendations based on continuous feedback from user interactions. Techniques such as Q-learning and deep Q-networks (DQNs) have been employed to balance exploration and exploitation, ensuring that the system remains responsive to evolving user preferences. In e-commerce and streaming services, reinforcement learning can dynamically adjust recommendations to maximize user retention and satisfaction, providing a personalized and adaptive user experience.

Scalability and performance optimization have remained critical considerations throughout the evolution of recommender systems. The increasing volume of data and the growing number of users necessitate efficient computational techniques and architectures. Distributed computing frameworks, parallelization, efficient data structures, and online learning algorithms are essential for managing large-scale data and ensuring real-time responsiveness. Techniques such as approximate nearest neighbor (ANN) search, model compression, and caching strategies reduce computational complexity and latency, enabling recommender systems to deliver timely and relevant recommendations at scale.

In conclusion, the historical evolution of recommender systems reflects a continuous journey of innovation and refinement, driven by the need to address the challenges of personalization and information overload in the digital age. From the early days of collaborative and content-based filtering to the integration of hybrid methods and the application of advanced machine learning techniques, recommender systems have undergone significant transformations. The advent of deep learning, attention mechanisms, and reinforcement learning has further elevated the capabilities of these systems, enabling them to capture complex user behaviors and deliver highly personalized recommendations. As the field continues to evolve, ongoing research and innovation will be essential to overcoming emerging challenges and unlocking new possibilities for enhancing user experience in an increasingly data-driven world.

2.2. Types of Recommender Systems

Recommender systems have become integral to the digital landscape, facilitating personalized experiences by suggesting products, services, and content tailored to individual preferences. The effectiveness of these systems hinges on the underlying recommendation algorithms, which can be broadly categorized into several types: collaborative filtering, content-based filtering, hybrid recommender systems, knowledge-based recommender systems, and context-aware recommender systems. Each type has distinct methodologies and applications, contributing uniquely to the overarching goal of enhancing user engagement and satisfaction.

Collaborative filtering, one of the earliest and most widely used approaches, operates on the principle that users who have agreed in the past will likely agree in the future. This method can be further divided into user-based and item-based collaborative filtering. User-based collaborative filtering identifies users with similar preferences to the target user and recommends items liked by these similar users. This involves calculating the similarity between users using metrics such as Pearson correlation coefficient or cosine similarity. For instance, the similarity $s(u,v)$ between users u and v can be expressed as:

$$s(u,v) = \frac{\sum_{i \in I_{uv}} r_{ui} r_{vi}}{\sqrt{\sum_{i \in I_u} r_{ui}^2} \sqrt{\sum_{i \in I_v} r_{vi}^2}}$$

where r_{ui} and r_{vi} are the ratings given by users u and v to item i, and I_{uv} is the set of items rated by both users. Item-based collaborative filtering, on the other hand, focuses on identifying items similar to those the target user has interacted with, employing similar similarity measures to compare items based on user ratings. For example, Amazon's recommendation engine famously uses item-based collaborative filtering to suggest products that are frequently bought together, enhancing the shopping experience by identifying patterns in purchasing behavior.

Content-based filtering, another fundamental approach, relies on the attributes of items to generate recommendations. This method constructs a profile for each user based on the features of items they have previously interacted with and recommends new items that share similar characteristics. For example, in a movie recommendation system, content-based filtering might analyze attributes such as genre, director, and actors to recommend movies similar to those the user has previously watched. The effectiveness of this approach depends on the quality and granularity of the item attributes, as well as the ability to accurately model user preferences. The use of techniques like Term Frequency-Inverse Document Frequency (TF-IDF) and word embeddings enhances the representation of textual attributes, enabling more precise content-based recommendations.

Hybrid recommender systems combine multiple recommendation techniques to leverage their respective strengths and mitigate their weaknesses. By integrating collaborative filtering and content-based filtering, hybrid systems can address issues such as the cold start problem and data sparsity, providing more robust and accurate recommendations. There are several ways to implement hybrid systems, including weighted hybrids, which combine the scores from different recommendation methods, and switching hybrids, which dynamically select the most appropriate method based on contextual factors. For instance, Netflix employs a sophisticated hybrid system that combines collaborative filtering, content-based filtering, and advanced machine learning models to deliver highly personalized movie and TV show recommendations, dynamically adapting to user preferences and behaviors.

Knowledge-based recommender systems are particularly useful in domains where user preferences are complex and not easily captured by collaborative or content-based methods. These systems leverage domain knowledge and user requirements to generate recommendations, often using rule-based or constraint-based approaches. For example, in a travel recommendation system, knowledge-based methods might consider user preferences for destination features, travel dates, and budget constraints to suggest suitable travel packages. The incorporation of expert knowledge and user-defined criteria ensures that the recommendations are highly relevant and tailored to specific needs, making this approach particularly effective for complex decision-making scenarios.

Context-aware recommender systems represent a more recent advancement, incorporating contextual information to enhance the relevance of recommendations. Contextual factors such as time, location, device type, and user activity can significantly influence user preferences and behaviors. By integrating this information, context-aware systems provide more personalized and timely recommendations. For example, a restaurant recommendation app might suggest dining options based on the user's current location and the time of day, offering contextually appropriate suggestions that enhance the user experience. The use of machine learning techniques to model and incorporate contextual variables further improves the accuracy and relevance of these recommendations.

The choice of recommender system type depends on the specific application domain and the nature of the available data. Collaborative filtering is highly effective in scenarios with rich user interaction data, such as e-commerce and social media platforms, where user preferences can be inferred from historical behavior. Content-based filtering excels in domains with well-defined item attributes, such as movie and music recommendations, where the characteristics of the items play a crucial role in user preferences. Hybrid systems are versatile and can be adapted to various contexts by combining the strengths of multiple approaches, making them suitable for complex and dynamic environments like online streaming services.

Knowledge-based and context-aware recommender systems are particularly valuable in domains where user preferences are intricate and context-sensitive. Knowledge-based methods provide precise recommendations in scenarios where user requirements are explicit and detailed, such as in personalized healthcare and financial services. Context-aware systems enhance the relevance of recommendations by considering the situational context, making them ideal for mobile and location-based services where user preferences vary based on contextual factors.

In conclusion, the diversity of recommender system types reflects the complexity and variability of user preferences and behaviors in the digital age. Each type of recommender system brings unique advantages and challenges, contributing to the overall goal of providing personalized and engaging user experiences. The ongoing development and integration of these systems, driven by advances in machine learning and artificial intelligence, continue to push the boundaries of what is possible in personalized recommendations. By understanding and leveraging the strengths of different recommendation approaches, developers can create sophisticated systems that meet the evolving needs and preferences of users across various domains, enhancing satisfaction and driving engagement in an increasingly interconnected world.

2.3. Basic Concepts and Terminology

Understanding the foundational concepts and terminology of recommender systems is crucial for delving into their design, implementation, and optimization. These systems, integral to modern digital platforms, operate through a complex interplay of algorithms, data structures, and evaluation metrics. This section elucidates the key concepts and terminology, providing a comprehensive framework to appreciate the nuances of recommender systems.

At the heart of recommender systems is the concept of **user-item interactions**, which represent the historical behavior of users towards various items. These interactions can take numerous forms, including explicit feedback like ratings and reviews, and implicit feedback such as clicks, views, and purchases. Explicit feedback provides direct indications of user preferences, often quantified on a numerical scale. For example, a rating matrix R can be defined where r_{ui} denotes the rating given by user u to item i. Implicit feedback, while more abundant, is less direct and typically requires additional processing to infer user preferences. For instance, the number of times a user listens to a song can be an indicator of their preference, though it lacks the clarity of explicit ratings.

The concept of **user and item profiles** is central to many recommendation algorithms. A user profile captures the preferences and behavior of a user, often represented as a vector of features derived from their interaction history. Similarly, an item profile encapsulates the attributes and characteristics of an item. In content-based filtering, these profiles are used to match users with items that have similar attributes.

For instance, in a movie recommendation system, a user profile might include preferences for genres, directors, and actors, while an item profile would detail the genre, director, and cast of a movie. The matching process involves calculating the similarity between user and item profiles using measures such as cosine similarity or Euclidean distance.

Similarity measures are fundamental to both collaborative filtering and content-based filtering. These measures quantify the likeness between users or items, guiding the recommendation process. Cosine similarity, for example, measures the cosine of the angle between two vectors in a multidimensional space, effectively capturing their orientation. Mathematically, the cosine similarity $sim(A, B)$ between two vectors A and B is given by:

$$sim(A, B) = \frac{A \cdot B}{\| A \| \| B \|} = \frac{\sum_{i=1}^{n} A_i B_i}{\sqrt{\sum_{i=1}^{n} A_i^2} \sqrt{\sum_{i=1}^{n} B_i^2}}$$

where $A \cdot B$ denotes the dot product, and $\| A \|$ and $\| B \|$ are the magnitudes of vectors A and B, respectively. Another common measure, Pearson correlation, assesses the linear relationship between users or items, normalizing for their mean and variance.

The **cold start problem** is a significant challenge in recommender systems, arising when new users or items have insufficient interaction data to generate reliable recommendations. This problem can be addressed through various strategies, such as leveraging content-based filtering to utilize item attributes or employing hybrid methods that combine multiple recommendation techniques. For instance, a new user on a streaming platform might be asked to select preferred genres and artists during the onboarding process, providing initial data to construct a user profile.

Data sparsity is another prevalent issue, especially in large-scale systems where the user-item interaction matrix is predominantly empty. Techniques such as matrix factorization and latent factor models are employed to mitigate data sparsity by reducing the dimensionality of the interaction matrix. Matrix factorization, for example, decomposes the interaction matrix R into two lower-dimensional matrices P and Q, where P represents user latent factors and Q represents item latent factors. The predicted rating $\hat{r}_{ui}$ for user u and item i is given by the dot product of their latent factor vectors:

$$\hat{r}_{ui} = P_u \cdot Q_i$$

This decomposition allows the system to infer missing values in the sparse interaction matrix, enhancing the accuracy of recommendations.

Evaluation metrics are essential for assessing the performance of recommender systems, ensuring that they meet user expectations and business objectives. Common metrics include precision, recall, F1-score, mean squared error (MSE), and root mean squared error (RMSE). Precision measures the proportion of relevant items among the recommended items, while recall assesses the proportion of relevant items that have been recommended out of all relevant items. F1-score, the harmonic mean of precision and recall, provides a balanced measure of both metrics. MSE and RMSE evaluate the accuracy of predicted ratings by comparing them with actual ratings, with lower values indicating better performance. For instance, RMSE is calculated as:

$$RMSE = \sqrt{\frac{1}{N}\sum_{u,i} (r_{ui} - \hat{r_{ui}})^2}$$

where N is the number of observed ratings, r_{ui} is the actual rating, and $\hat{r}_{ui}$ is the predicted rating.

Hybrid recommender systems integrate multiple recommendation techniques to leverage their respective strengths and mitigate their weaknesses. These systems can combine collaborative filtering, content-based filtering, and other approaches in various ways. For example, a weighted hybrid system might combine the scores from collaborative and content-based methods using a weighted sum:

$$Score(u, i) = w_1 \times CF\ Score(u, i) + w_2 \times CB\ Score(u, i)$$

where w_1 and w_2 are the weights assigned to the collaborative filtering (CF) and content-based (CB) scores, respectively. Hybrid systems are particularly effective in addressing challenges such as the cold start problem and data sparsity, providing a more robust and accurate recommendation framework.

Context-aware recommender systems incorporate contextual information, such as time, location, device type, and user activity, to enhance the relevance of recommendations. These systems model the impact of context on user preferences and behaviors, providing more personalized and timely suggestions. For instance, a restaurant recommendation app might use the user's current location and the time of day to suggest nearby dining options. The integration of contextual variables can be achieved using various machine learning techniques, including feature engineering and contextual bandit algorithms, which dynamically adjust recommendations based on real-time context.

In conclusion, the basic concepts and terminology of recommender systems provide a comprehensive framework for understanding their design and functionality. User-item interactions, similarity measures, evaluation metrics, and hybrid approaches are fundamental to the operation of these systems, enabling them to deliver personalized and relevant recommendations. Addressing challenges such as the cold start problem and data sparsity through advanced techniques like matrix factorization and context-aware recommendations ensures that recommender systems remain effective and responsive to user needs. As the field continues to evolve, a deep understanding of these foundational concepts will be essential for developing sophisticated and impactful recommender systems that enhance user experience and drive engagement in an increasingly digital world.

2.4. Overview of Common Algorithms

The effectiveness of recommender systems hinges on the algorithms that drive their ability to predict user preferences and deliver personalized recommendations. A myriad of algorithms, each with its unique approach and underlying principles, has been developed to address the diverse needs of recommendation tasks. This section provides an overview of the most common algorithms used in recommender systems, discussing their mechanisms, strengths, and potential limitations.

Collaborative filtering remains one of the cornerstone methodologies in the realm of recommender systems. This approach is predicated on the idea that users who have agreed in their past preferences will continue to agree in the future. Collaborative filtering can be divided into two primary types: user-based and item-based collaborative filtering. User-based collaborative filtering involves identifying a target user's nearest neighbors (i.e., users with similar preferences) and recommending items that these neighbors have liked. Mathematically, the similarity between users is often computed using measures such as cosine similarity or Pearson correlation. For example, cosine similarity between two users u and v is given by:

$$sim(u, v) = \frac{\sum_{i \in I_{uv}} r_{ui} r_{vi}}{\sqrt{\sum_{i \in I_u} r_{ui}^2} \sqrt{\sum_{i \in I_v} r_{vi}^2}}$$

where r_{ui} and r_{vi} represent the ratings of users u and v for item i, and I_{uv} is the set of items rated by both users. Item-based collaborative filtering, on the other hand, focuses on the similarity between items. It recommends items similar to those the user has interacted with, using similar similarity measures applied to the item profiles.

Matrix factorization techniques, such as Singular Value Decomposition (SVD) and Alternating Least Squares (ALS), have significantly advanced the capabilities of collaborative filtering. These techniques decompose the user-item interaction matrix into lower-dimensional latent factors, revealing underlying patterns in the data. For instance, the interaction matrix R can be approximated by the product of two lower-dimensional matrices P (user latent factors) and Q (item latent factors):

$$R \approx PQ^T$$

The predicted rating $\hat{r}_{ui}$ for user u and item i is then given by the dot product of their respective latent factor vectors:

$$\hat{r}_{ui} = P_u \cdot Q_i$$

Matrix factorization excels in capturing the latent structures in the data, making it effective for generating accurate recommendations, especially in the presence of sparse data.

Content-based filtering algorithms rely on the attributes of items to recommend similar items to those a user has previously liked. This approach involves constructing a profile for each user based on the features of items they have interacted with. For example, in a movie recommendation system, content-based filtering might analyze attributes such as genre, director, and actors. The similarity between the user profile and item profile can be computed using measures like cosine similarity. If a user frequently watches science fiction movies directed by a particular director, the system will recommend other science fiction movies or works by the same director. This method is particularly effective in scenarios with rich item metadata but can suffer from overspecialization, where the system repeatedly recommends items too similar to those already consumed.

Hybrid recommender systems integrate multiple recommendation algorithms to leverage their respective strengths and mitigate their weaknesses. These systems can combine collaborative filtering, content-based filtering, and other methods in various ways. A common hybrid approach is the weighted hybrid, which combines the scores from different recommendation techniques using a weighted sum:

$$Score(u, i) = w_1 \times CF\ Score(u, i) + w_2 \times CB\ Score(u, i)$$

where w_1 and w_2 are the weights assigned to the collaborative filtering (CF) and content-based (CB) scores, respectively. Another approach is the switching hybrid, which dynamically selects the most appropriate recommendation method based on specific criteria, such as the amount of user interaction data available. Hybrid systems can address the cold start problem, data sparsity, and overspecialization, providing a more robust and versatile recommendation framework.

Neural collaborative filtering is an advanced technique that employs deep learning to capture complex, non-linear relationships in the data. This method uses neural networks to learn high-dimensional embeddings for users and items, enhancing the representation of latent factors. A typical neural collaborative filtering model might involve a multi-layer perceptron (MLP) to model the interaction between user and item embeddings. The final recommendation score is derived from the output of the neural network, which combines the learned embeddings in a non-linear fashion:

$$\hat{r}_{ui} = MLP(\mathbf{p}_u, \mathbf{q}_i)$$

where $\mathbf{p}_u$ and $\mathbf{q}_i$ are the embeddings for user u and item i, respectively. Neural collaborative filtering has been shown to outperform traditional matrix factorization techniques by capturing more intricate patterns in the data.

Convolutional neural networks (CNNs) and **recurrent neural networks (RNNs)** have also been adapted for recommender systems, particularly in processing unstructured data such as images, text, and sequential interactions. CNNs are effective in analyzing visual content, making them suitable for recommendations based on image similarity. For example, a fashion recommendation system might use CNNs to analyze product images and recommend visually similar items. RNNs, especially their advanced variants like Long Short-Term Memory (LSTM) networks, are adept at modeling sequential data, capturing temporal dependencies in user interactions. This capability is crucial in applications such as music or video streaming services, where the order and timing of interactions provide valuable insights into user preferences.

Autoencoders, particularly variational autoencoders (VAEs), are used for dimensionality reduction and feature learning in recommender systems. Autoencoders compress the input data into a lower-dimensional latent space and then reconstruct it, capturing essential patterns while filtering out noise. In recommendation tasks, autoencoders can be used to learn compact representations of user-item interactions, which are then used to generate recommendations. VAEs further enhance this capability by learning a distribution over the latent space, allowing for the generation of new, plausible user-item interactions.

In conclusion, the landscape of recommender system algorithms is rich and varied, encompassing a wide range of techniques from collaborative and content-based filtering to advanced deep learning methods. Each algorithm brings unique advantages and challenges, contributing to the overall goal of providing personalized and accurate recommendations. Collaborative filtering and matrix factorization excel in capturing latent structures in user-item interactions, while content-based filtering leverages item attributes to align recommendations with user preferences. Hybrid systems combine multiple methods to enhance robustness and address specific challenges, and neural networks introduce powerful capabilities for learning complex, high-dimensional representations. As the field continues to evolve, ongoing research and innovation will be essential to further refine these algorithms and develop new approaches that enhance the effectiveness and applicability of recommender systems in an increasingly data-driven world.

2.5. Conclusion

The exploration of recommender systems reveals a rich tapestry of methodologies, each designed to address the complex and multifaceted nature of predicting user preferences in a digital landscape characterized by information overload. From their historical roots in collaborative and content-based filtering, recommender systems have evolved significantly, driven by the need to enhance personalization and improve user engagement. This evolution has been marked by the integration of hybrid systems, the application of sophisticated machine learning techniques, and the continual refinement of algorithms to handle the challenges of data sparsity, cold start problems, and scalability.

Collaborative filtering, as one of the earliest methods, capitalized on the power of collective user preferences to generate recommendations. By identifying patterns in user behavior, collaborative filtering systems could suggest items that users with similar tastes had enjoyed. This method, exemplified by techniques such as user-based and item-based collaborative filtering, laid the foundation for more advanced approaches. However, its reliance on user interaction data made it vulnerable to the cold start problem and data sparsity, necessitating the development of complementary methods.

Content-based filtering emerged as a solution to some of these challenges by focusing on the attributes of items. This approach constructs detailed profiles for users based on the features of items they have interacted with, recommending new items that share similar characteristics. While content-based filtering is effective in domains with rich item metadata, it often suffers from overspecialization, where recommendations become too similar to past preferences, limiting the diversity of suggestions.

The advent of hybrid recommender systems marked a significant advancement, combining the strengths of multiple methods to create more robust and accurate recommendations. By integrating collaborative filtering, content-based filtering, and other techniques, hybrid systems address the limitations of individual approaches. They provide a versatile framework that can adapt to various contexts and user behaviors, offering a balanced solution to the cold start problem and data sparsity. Netflix's recommendation engine, which seamlessly blends multiple methods, stands as a testament to the efficacy of hybrid systems in real-world applications.

The incorporation of machine learning and deep learning has further revolutionized recommender systems. Matrix factorization techniques such as Singular Value Decomposition (SVD) and Alternating Least Squares (ALS) decompose the user-item interaction matrix into latent factors, capturing underlying patterns and improving recommendation accuracy. Deep learning models, including neural collaborative filtering, convolutional neural networks (CNNs), and recurrent neural networks (RNNs), introduce powerful capabilities for learning complex, non-linear relationships and processing unstructured data. These models have demonstrated remarkable success in enhancing the precision and personalization of recommendations.

Attention mechanisms and reinforcement learning represent the forefront of innovation in recommender systems. Attention mechanisms, particularly self-attention used in transformer models, allow systems to dynamically focus on the most relevant parts of the input data, capturing long-range dependencies and contextual relevance. This capability enhances the accuracy of recommendations in applications such as personalized news feeds. Reinforcement learning frames the recommendation process as a sequential decision-making problem, optimizing for long-term user engagement and satisfaction. Techniques such as Q-learning and deep Q-networks (DQNs) enable recommender systems to adapt to evolving user preferences, providing a dynamic and personalized user experience.

Scalability and performance optimization remain critical considerations in the practical deployment of recommender systems. The increasing volume of data and the growing number of users necessitate efficient computational techniques and architectures. Distributed computing frameworks, parallelization, efficient data structures, and online learning algorithms are essential for managing large-scale data and ensuring real-time responsiveness. Techniques such as approximate nearest neighbor (ANN) search, model compression, and caching strategies reduce computational complexity and latency, enabling recommender systems to deliver timely and relevant recommendations at scale.

In summary, the landscape of recommender systems is characterized by continuous innovation and refinement. The integration of collaborative and content-based filtering, the development of hybrid systems, and the application of advanced machine learning techniques have significantly enhanced the ability of these systems to deliver personalized and accurate recommendations. The ongoing evolution of recommender systems, driven by advancements in deep learning, attention mechanisms, and reinforcement learning, promises to further elevate their capabilities, ensuring that they remain at the forefront of personalization technologies. As the digital world continues to expand, the role of recommender systems in enhancing user experience and engagement will only become more critical, underscoring the importance of continued research and development in this dynamic field. Through a deep understanding of the foundational principles and the latest advancements, developers can create sophisticated recommender systems that meet the evolving needs and preferences of users, driving engagement and satisfaction in an increasingly interconnected and data-driven world.

3. Data Preprocessing for Recommender Systems

In the realm of recommender systems, data is the cornerstone of success. The quality and preprocessing of data play a pivotal role in determining the effectiveness and accuracy of recommendations. Data preprocessing involves transforming raw data into a suitable format for recommendation algorithms, ensuring that the input data is both reliable and relevant. This chapter delves into the essential steps and techniques for data preprocessing, covering data collection, cleaning, feature engineering, handling missing data, and scaling.

3.1. Data Collection Techniques

The efficacy of recommender systems fundamentally hinges on the quality and comprehensiveness of the data they leverage. Data collection techniques are thus a critical aspect of recommender system development, as they provide the raw material from which preferences and patterns are discerned. Effective data collection encompasses various methodologies, each tailored to capture specific types of user interactions and contextual information. This section delves into the primary techniques for collecting data, highlighting their significance, challenges, and implications for recommendation accuracy and personalization.

One of the primary sources of data for recommender systems is **explicit feedback**, which includes direct user inputs such as ratings, reviews, and preferences. Explicit feedback is invaluable as it provides clear indications of user preferences, allowing for precise modeling and recommendation. For instance, in a movie recommendation system, users might rate films on a scale from one to five stars. These ratings can be compiled into a user-item interaction matrix, where each entry r_{ui} represents the rating given by user u to item i. Such a matrix forms the backbone of collaborative filtering techniques, where the goal is to predict missing entries based on observed ratings. However, obtaining explicit feedback can be challenging due to the reliance on user participation, which may be sporadic or biased, thus limiting the data's comprehensiveness and representativeness.

In contrast, **implicit feedback** involves capturing user interactions that are indicative of preferences but are not explicitly stated. Examples of implicit feedback include clicks, page views, purchase history, and dwell time on content. Implicit feedback is often more abundant than explicit feedback, providing a richer dataset for analysis. For example, an e-commerce platform might track which products users click on, add to their cart, or purchase. This data can be used to infer preferences and build user profiles without requiring direct input from users. However, implicit feedback can be noisy and ambiguous, as not all interactions necessarily reflect positive preferences. For instance, a user might click on a product out of curiosity rather than genuine interest, necessitating sophisticated filtering and weighting techniques to accurately interpret the data.

Contextual information is another crucial dimension in data collection, enhancing the relevance of recommendations by considering the situational context of user interactions. Contextual data can include time of day, location, device type, and user activity. For example, a music streaming service might recommend different types of music based on the time of day, suggesting upbeat tracks in the morning and relaxing tunes in the evening. Collecting contextual information often involves integrating data from various sources, such as GPS for location tracking or system logs for device usage patterns. The incorporation of contextual data enables context-aware recommender systems to deliver more personalized and timely suggestions, though it also raises concerns about data privacy and the need for robust mechanisms to protect user information.

User profiles and **demographic data** are essential for enriching the dataset used by recommender systems. User profiles typically include demographic information such as age, gender, income level, and education, as well as psychographic data like interests, attitudes, and lifestyle preferences. This information can be gathered through registration forms, surveys, or third-party data providers. Demographic data helps segment users into meaningful groups, allowing for more targeted recommendations. For instance, a book recommendation system might use demographic data to suggest different genres to teenagers compared to middle-aged users. While demographic data can enhance personalization, it also requires careful handling to avoid stereotyping and ensure fairness in recommendations.

Social data has become increasingly important with the rise of social media and online communities. Social data includes information about users' social connections, interactions, and shared content. For example, a social media platform might analyze users' friend networks, likes, shares, and comments to infer preferences and recommend content that is popular within their social circles. Social recommender systems leverage this data to enhance the relevance and social validation of recommendations, as users are often influenced by the preferences and behaviors of their peers. However, social data can be complex to analyze due to its dynamic and interconnected nature, necessitating advanced graph-based algorithms and network analysis techniques.

Transactional data is particularly relevant for e-commerce and financial services, where purchase history, transaction amounts, and payment methods provide valuable insights into user preferences and spending behavior. For instance, an online retailer can analyze purchase patterns to recommend complementary products or identify trends such as seasonal buying habits. Transactional data is typically structured and voluminous, making it well-suited for machine learning algorithms that require large datasets for training. However, the sensitive nature of transactional data also demands stringent security measures to protect user privacy and comply with regulatory requirements.

The integration of data from **multiple sources** is often necessary to build comprehensive and accurate recommender systems. For example, a travel recommendation system might combine explicit feedback from user reviews, implicit feedback from browsing behavior, contextual data from GPS and weather forecasts, and transactional data from booking histories. This multi-source data fusion enhances the richness and robustness of the dataset, enabling more sophisticated and contextually relevant recommendations. However, integrating heterogeneous data sources poses challenges in terms of data compatibility, quality, and preprocessing.

Data preprocessing is a critical step in the data collection process, ensuring that the collected data is clean, consistent, and suitable for analysis. This involves tasks such as data cleaning, which addresses issues like missing values, duplicates, and inconsistencies; data normalization, which standardizes the scale of features; and data transformation, which converts raw data into a format suitable for modeling. Effective preprocessing enhances the quality of the input data, thereby improving the accuracy and reliability of the recommendations generated by the system.

In conclusion, the techniques for data collection in recommender systems are diverse and multifaceted, reflecting the complexity of capturing user preferences and behaviors in a digital environment. Explicit and implicit feedback, contextual information, user profiles, social data, transactional data, and multi-source integration each contribute uniquely to the data landscape, providing the raw material necessary for building robust and personalized recommendation models. The effectiveness of these techniques hinges on their ability to capture relevant and accurate data while addressing challenges related to data noise, ambiguity, privacy, and integration. As the field of recommender systems continues to evolve, innovative data collection methodologies and advanced preprocessing techniques will remain critical to enhancing the precision and personalization of recommendations, ultimately driving user engagement and satisfaction in an increasingly data-driven world.

3.2. Data Cleaning and Preparation

The process of data cleaning and preparation is pivotal in the development of effective recommender systems, as it ensures that the raw data collected from various sources is transformed into a high-quality, consistent, and analyzable format. This process is fundamental to the performance of recommendation algorithms, as the presence of noise, inconsistencies, and missing values can significantly degrade the accuracy and reliability of the recommendations. Data cleaning and preparation involve several critical steps, including data cleaning, data integration, data transformation, and data reduction, each of which plays a vital role in refining the dataset for subsequent analysis and modeling.

Data cleaning is the first and perhaps most crucial step in the preparation process, addressing issues such as missing values, duplicates, and outliers. Missing data can arise from various sources, including user omission, system errors, or data extraction processes. Strategies to handle missing values include imputation, where missing entries are filled in using statistical methods, such as the mean, median, or mode of the available data, or more sophisticated techniques like k-nearest neighbors (KNN) imputation and machine learning models trained to predict missing values. For instance, in a user-item interaction matrix where user ratings are missing, matrix factorization techniques can be employed to estimate the missing entries based on the observed data.

$$\hat{r}_{ui} = P_u \cdot Q_i$$

where $\hat{r}_{ui}$ is the predicted rating for user u and item i, and P and Q are the user and item latent factor matrices, respectively.

Duplicate records, another common issue, can distort data analysis and must be identified and removed. This involves techniques such as fuzzy matching, which detects similar but not identical records based on string matching algorithms like Levenshtein distance. Outliers, or anomalous data points, can skew the results of statistical analyses and machine learning models. Detecting and handling outliers involves statistical methods such as Z-score, IQR (Interquartile Range), and robust clustering algorithms that identify and mitigate the impact of these anomalies on the dataset.

Data integration is essential when combining data from multiple sources, ensuring consistency and eliminating redundancy. This step is particularly important in complex systems where data originates from various databases, applications, or sensors. Schema integration, a key aspect of this process, involves aligning the data structures from different sources to form a unified view. For instance, in an e-commerce recommender system, user data might be collected from website interactions, mobile app usage, and social media platforms. Integrating these diverse data sources requires resolving schema conflicts, such as differences in data formats, attribute names, and data types. Techniques like entity resolution and data deduplication are employed to ensure that the integrated data is coherent and free from redundancies.

Data transformation encompasses the tasks of data normalization, standardization, and feature engineering, which are critical for preparing data for machine learning algorithms. Normalization involves scaling the data to a specific range, often between 0 and 1, to ensure that no single feature dominates the others due to differences in scale. Standardization, on the other hand, involves rescaling the data to have a mean of zero and a standard deviation of one, which is particularly useful for algorithms that assume normally distributed data. For example, in a dataset containing user ratings on different scales, standardizing the ratings ensures that they are comparable across users and items:

$$z = \frac{x - \mu}{\sigma}$$

where z is the standardized value, x is the original value, μ is the mean, and σ is the standard deviation.

Feature engineering is the process of creating new features or modifying existing ones to enhance the predictive power of the models. This includes creating interaction features, polynomial features, or aggregating features over time. For instance, in a music recommendation system, additional features such as the average listening duration, frequency of listening, and temporal patterns (e.g., listening habits during weekdays versus weekends) can provide valuable insights into user preferences and improve the accuracy of the recommendations.

Data reduction techniques are employed to reduce the complexity and dimensionality of the dataset while retaining its essential characteristics. This is crucial for improving the efficiency and scalability of machine learning algorithms, especially when dealing with large-scale datasets. Principal Component Analysis (PCA) is a widely used dimensionality reduction technique that transforms the original high-dimensional data into a lower-dimensional space by identifying the principal components that capture the most variance in the data. Similarly, feature selection methods such as Recursive Feature Elimination (RFE) and Lasso regression can be used to identify and retain the most relevant features, discarding those that contribute little to the predictive power of the model.

$$\mathbf{X} = \mathbf{WZ} + \boldsymbol{\mu}$$

where $\mathbf{X}$ is the original data matrix, $\mathbf{W}$ is the matrix of principal components, $\mathbf{Z}$ is the matrix of principal component scores, and $\boldsymbol{\mu}$ is the mean of the original data.

Data validation and consistency checking are final steps in the data preparation process, ensuring that the cleaned and transformed data meets the required quality standards. Validation techniques include cross-validation, where the data is split into training and testing sets to assess the performance of the model, and consistency checks, which verify that the data adheres to defined rules and constraints. For example, in a user-item interaction matrix, consistency checks might involve verifying that user IDs and item IDs are within valid ranges and that there are no invalid or contradictory entries.

The implications of effective data cleaning and preparation are profound, as they directly influence the performance and reliability of recommender systems. High-quality data ensures that the models can accurately capture user preferences and behaviors, leading to more precise and personalized recommendations. Conversely, poor data quality can lead to biased, inaccurate, and untrustworthy recommendations, undermining user satisfaction and engagement. Therefore, investing in robust data cleaning and preparation processes is essential for the success of recommender systems, as it lays the foundation for building models that can deliver valuable and relevant insights.

In conclusion, data cleaning and preparation are critical components of the recommender system development pipeline, involving a series of meticulous steps to transform raw data into a high-quality, analyzable format. From addressing missing values and duplicates to integrating data from multiple sources, transforming and reducing the data, and validating its quality, each step plays a vital role in ensuring that the dataset is ready for effective modeling. The success of recommender systems hinges on the quality of the input data, making data cleaning and preparation indispensable for achieving accurate, reliable, and personalized recommendations. As the complexity and volume of data continue to grow, advancements in data preparation techniques will remain essential for enhancing the performance and scalability of recommender systems in an increasingly data-driven world.

3.3. Dealing with Outliers

Outliers present a significant challenge in data preparation for recommender systems, as they can distort statistical analyses and degrade the performance of machine learning models. Outliers are data points that deviate markedly from the overall pattern of the data, potentially arising from various sources such as data entry errors, measurement errors, or genuine but rare events. Effectively identifying and managing outliers is crucial to ensure the robustness and reliability of the recommender systems, as unaddressed outliers can lead to biased models and inaccurate recommendations. This section delves into the methodologies for detecting and handling outliers, emphasizing their importance and the implications for recommender systems.

The detection of outliers is the first step in managing their impact. Several statistical and machine learning techniques are available for this purpose, each suited to different types of data and contexts. **Univariate methods** focus on detecting outliers within a single variable. Common approaches include the Z-score method and the Interquartile Range (IQR) method. The Z-score method identifies outliers by calculating the number of standard deviations a data point is from the mean:

$$Z = \frac{X - \mu}{\sigma}$$

where Z is the Z-score, X is the value of the data point, μ is the mean, and σ is the standard deviation. Data points with a Z-score beyond a certain threshold (typically ± 3) are considered outliers. The IQR method identifies outliers based on the spread of the middle 50% of the data. The IQR is calculated as the difference between the third quartile (Q3) and the first quartile (Q1):

$$IQR = Q3 - Q1$$

Outliers are then defined as data points that fall below $Q1 - 1.5 \times$ IQR or above $Q3 + 1.5 \times$ IQR.

Multivariate methods consider the relationships between multiple variables to detect outliers. Techniques such as Mahalanobis distance and principal component analysis (PCA) are commonly used. Mahalanobis distance measures the distance between a data point and the mean of the distribution, accounting for correlations between variables:

$$D_M(\mathbf{x}) = \sqrt{(\mathbf{x} - \boldsymbol{\mu})^\mathsf{T} \mathbf{S}^{-1}(\mathbf{x} - \boldsymbol{\mu})}$$

where $D_M(\mathbf{x})$ is the Mahalanobis distance, $\mathbf{x}$ is the data point, $\boldsymbol{\mu}$ is the mean vector, and $\mathbf{S}$ is the covariance matrix. Data points with a high Mahalanobis distance are considered outliers. PCA, on the other hand, reduces the dimensionality of the data and identifies outliers based on their projection onto the principal components.

Machine learning-based methods leverage algorithms designed to identify outliers as part of their modeling process. Isolation forests and One-Class SVMs are prominent examples. Isolation forests work by recursively partitioning the data, with the assumption that outliers are easier to isolate due to their rarity. Each partitioning step splits the data based on randomly chosen attributes and values, and outliers tend to be isolated with fewer partitions:

$$Anomaly\ Score(\mathbf{x}) = 2^{-\frac{E(h(\mathbf{x}))}{c(n)}}$$

where $E(h(\mathbf{x}))$ is the average path length of the data point $\mathbf{x}$ in the isolation forest, and $c(n)$ is a normalization constant. One-Class SVMs, in contrast, learn a boundary that separates normal data points from outliers based on their distribution in the feature space.

Once identified, the treatment of outliers involves deciding whether to remove, modify, or retain them based on their nature and the context of the analysis. **Removal of outliers** is a straightforward approach but should be done cautiously, especially when the outliers might represent significant and meaningful anomalies. For instance, in a financial recommender system, unusually high transaction amounts might be rare but important for identifying high-value customers or fraud detection. Therefore, it is crucial to balance the need for a clean dataset with the preservation of potentially valuable information.

Modification of outliers involves techniques such as winsorization, where extreme values are replaced with the nearest non-outlying values, or transformation, where outliers are brought closer to the central tendency of the data through mathematical transformations like log transformation or Box-Cox transformation. For example, log transformation can be particularly effective in reducing the impact of high positive outliers in skewed distributions:

$$Y' = \log(Y + 1)$$

where Y is the original value and Y' is the transformed value.

In some cases, **retention of outliers** is necessary when they provide critical insights or when the context of the analysis requires their inclusion. For instance, in anomaly detection systems, the identification and understanding of outliers are central to the system's functionality. In such scenarios, rather than removing or modifying outliers, the focus shifts to understanding their characteristics and underlying causes.

The implications of effectively dealing with outliers in recommender systems are significant. Properly managed outliers ensure that the models built on the data are robust and reliable, leading to accurate and personalized recommendations. Conversely, neglecting outliers can result in biased models that produce suboptimal recommendations, negatively impacting user satisfaction and engagement. Furthermore, the techniques used to detect and handle outliers must be chosen and applied judiciously, considering the specific context and objectives of the recommender system.

In conclusion, dealing with outliers is a critical aspect of data preparation for recommender systems, requiring a combination of statistical, machine learning, and domain-specific techniques. From detecting outliers using univariate and multivariate methods to deciding on their treatment based on the context, each step plays a vital role in ensuring the quality and reliability of the dataset. The careful management of outliers enhances the robustness and accuracy of recommender systems, ultimately leading to better user experiences and more effective personalization. As the complexity and volume of data continue to grow, advanced outlier detection and handling techniques will remain essential for maintaining the integrity and performance of recommender systems in an increasingly data-driven world.

3.4. Feature Engineering

Feature engineering is a pivotal step in the development of recommender systems, involving the creation, transformation, and selection of variables that enhance the predictive power of machine learning models. It is the process of using domain knowledge to extract meaningful features from raw data, thereby improving the system's ability to discern patterns and make accurate recommendations. Effective feature engineering can significantly impact the performance of recommender systems by highlighting relevant aspects of the data, reducing noise, and enabling models to better capture the underlying structure of user preferences and item characteristics.

The first step in feature engineering is **feature creation**, where new features are derived from existing data. This process often involves combining or transforming raw data into forms that are more suitable for modeling. For instance, in a movie recommendation system, basic features such as the genre, director, and cast of a movie can be augmented with additional features like the average rating, the number of ratings, and the release year. Temporal features, such as the time of day or the day of the week when a user interacts with content, can also provide valuable insights. For example, if a user frequently watches certain genres during the weekend, this temporal pattern can be captured as a feature to improve the relevance of recommendations.

Interaction features are another important aspect of feature creation. These features capture the relationships between different variables, often revealing patterns that are not apparent from the individual features alone. For example, in an e-commerce recommendation system, interaction features might include the combination of user demographics and item attributes, such as the interaction between a user's age group and the product category. These interaction terms can be created through techniques such as polynomial feature generation, where features are combined multiplicatively to capture their joint effect:

$$Interaction\ Feature = x_1 \times x_2$$

where x_1 and x_2 are individual features. This approach allows the model to account for complex interactions and dependencies between variables, enhancing its predictive power.

Feature transformation involves modifying existing features to make them more suitable for modeling. Common transformations include scaling, normalization, and encoding. Scaling and normalization are particularly important for algorithms that are sensitive to the scale of the data, such as gradient-based optimization methods used in neural networks. Normalization typically involves rescaling the data to a specific range, often between 0 and 1, using the min-max scaling method:

$$x' = \frac{x - \min(x)}{\max(x) - \min(x)}$$

where x is the original value and x' is the normalized value. Standardization, another common transformation, involves rescaling the data to have a mean of zero and a standard deviation of one:

$$z = \frac{x - \mu}{\sigma}$$

where μ is the mean and σ is the standard deviation of the original data. These transformations ensure that the features are on a comparable scale, which can improve the convergence and performance of machine learning algorithms.

Encoding categorical variables is another crucial aspect of feature transformation. Categorical variables, such as user gender or product category, need to be converted into numerical representations that can be processed by machine learning models. Common encoding techniques include one-hot encoding and ordinal encoding. One-hot encoding transforms categorical variables into binary vectors, where each category is represented by a separate binary feature. For example, a categorical variable with three levels (e.g., "red," "green," "blue") can be transformed into three binary features:

$$Red = [1,0,0], \; Green = [0,1,0], \; Blue = [0,0,1]$$

Ordinal encoding, on the other hand, assigns a unique integer to each category, which is particularly useful for ordinal variables where the categories have a natural order.

Feature selection is the process of identifying the most relevant features for the model, reducing the dimensionality of the dataset while retaining its predictive power. This step is crucial for enhancing the efficiency and performance of the model, as redundant or irrelevant features can introduce noise and reduce the model's generalization ability. Feature selection techniques can be broadly categorized into filter methods, wrapper methods, and embedded methods. Filter methods, such as correlation analysis and mutual information, assess the relevance of features based on statistical criteria. Wrapper methods, such as recursive feature elimination (RFE), involve training the model with different subsets of features and selecting the subset that yields the best performance. Embedded methods, such as Lasso regression and tree-based algorithms, incorporate feature selection as part of the model training process by penalizing the inclusion of less important features.

Dimensionality reduction techniques, such as Principal Component Analysis (PCA) and t-Distributed Stochastic Neighbor Embedding (t-SNE), are also employed to reduce the number of features while preserving the essential structure of the data. PCA transforms the original features into a set of orthogonal components that capture the maximum variance in the data:

$$\mathbf{X} = \mathbf{WZ} + \boldsymbol{\mu}$$

where $\mathbf{X}$ is the original data matrix, $\mathbf{W}$ is the matrix of principal components, $\mathbf{Z}$ is the matrix of principal component scores, and $\boldsymbol{\mu}$ is the mean of the original data. t-SNE, on the other hand, is particularly useful for visualizing high-dimensional data by projecting it into a lower-dimensional space while preserving the local structure of the data.

The implications of effective feature engineering are profound, as it directly impacts the accuracy, interpretability, and performance of recommender systems. Well-engineered features enable models to capture the underlying patterns in the data more effectively, leading to more accurate and personalized recommendations. Conversely, poor feature engineering can result in models that fail to generalize well, produce biased predictions, or overlook important aspects of user preferences and item characteristics. Therefore, investing in thorough and thoughtful feature engineering is essential for the success of recommender systems.

In conclusion, feature engineering is a critical and intricate process that involves creating, transforming, and selecting features to enhance the predictive power of machine learning models. Through techniques such as interaction feature generation, scaling, normalization, encoding, and dimensionality reduction, feature engineering transforms raw data into a form that can be effectively utilized by recommender systems. The success of these systems hinges on the quality of the features, making feature engineering an indispensable step in the development pipeline. As the complexity and volume of data continue to grow, advanced feature engineering techniques will remain essential for building sophisticated and effective recommender systems that deliver accurate, relevant, and personalized recommendations in an increasingly data-driven world.

3.5. Handling Sparse Data

Sparse data is a prevalent challenge in recommender systems, arising when the user-item interaction matrix contains a large proportion of missing values. This sparsity is typical in large-scale systems where users interact with only a small subset of available items, leading to a matrix that is mostly empty. Handling sparse data effectively is crucial for the performance and reliability of recommender systems, as it directly impacts the accuracy and coverage of recommendations. Various techniques have been developed to address this issue, including matrix factorization, imputation methods, and hybrid models, each contributing uniquely to mitigating the effects of sparsity.

The user-item interaction matrix is central to collaborative filtering methods, where the rows represent users, the columns represent items, and the entries represent interactions, such as ratings or clicks. In a typical scenario, the matrix is sparse because most users interact with a limited number of items. For example, a movie recommendation system might have millions of users and thousands of movies, but each user has only rated a small fraction of the total available movies. This sparsity can hinder the ability of collaborative filtering algorithms to identify meaningful patterns and similarities, necessitating strategies to address it.

Matrix factorization is one of the most effective techniques for handling sparse data. It decomposes the sparse user-item interaction matrix into two lower-dimensional matrices, representing the latent factors of users and items. The goal is to approximate the original matrix by capturing the underlying structure in these latent factors. Singular Value Decomposition (SVD) and Alternating Least Squares (ALS) are widely used matrix factorization techniques. In SVD, the interaction matrix R is decomposed into three matrices:

$$R \approx U\Sigma V^T$$

where U and V are orthogonal matrices representing user and item latent factors, respectively, and Σ is a diagonal matrix of singular values. The product of these matrices reconstructs the original matrix, filling in the missing values with estimated interactions based on the latent factors. ALS, on the other hand, iteratively optimizes the user and item matrices by alternating between fixing one matrix and solving for the other, minimizing the reconstruction error. These methods not only handle sparsity effectively but also uncover hidden patterns in user preferences and item characteristics, leading to more accurate recommendations.

Imputation methods provide another approach to dealing with sparse data by filling in the missing values in the interaction matrix. These methods can range from simple strategies, such as using the global average rating or user/item averages, to more sophisticated techniques like k-nearest neighbors (KNN) imputation and machine learning models. KNN imputation, for example, estimates missing values based on the ratings of similar users or items. If user u has not rated item i, the missing rating r_{ui} can be imputed using the ratings from the k most similar users who have rated item i:

$$r_{ui} = \frac{\sum_{v \in N_k(u)} s(u, v) r_{vi}}{\sum_{v \in N_k(u)} s(u, v)}$$

where $N_k(u)$ is the set of the k nearest neighbors of user u who have rated item i, and $s(u, v)$ is the similarity between users u and v. While imputation methods can help alleviate sparsity, they may introduce bias if the imputed values do not accurately reflect user preferences.

Hybrid models combine multiple recommendation techniques to leverage their strengths and mitigate the limitations associated with sparse data. For instance, hybrid models can integrate collaborative filtering with content-based filtering, using item attributes to enhance recommendations when user interaction data is sparse. This approach can be particularly effective in cold start scenarios, where new users or items have little interaction data. By utilizing content-based features, such as item descriptions, tags, and metadata, the system can generate initial recommendations that are refined as more interaction data becomes available. Netflix, for example, employs a hybrid approach that combines collaborative filtering, content-based filtering, and machine learning models to provide personalized movie recommendations, even for new users and items.

Dimensionality reduction techniques, such as Principal Component Analysis (PCA) and Non-negative Matrix Factorization (NMF), are also valuable for handling sparse data. These methods reduce the number of dimensions in the interaction matrix while preserving its essential structure, making it easier to identify patterns and similarities. PCA transforms the original data into a set of orthogonal components that capture the most variance, effectively condensing the information into a lower-dimensional space. NMF, which constrains the latent factors to be non-negative, provides interpretable results that can be more intuitive for understanding user and item characteristics.

$$\mathbf{X} \approx \mathbf{WH}$$

where $\mathbf{X}$ is the original interaction matrix, $\mathbf{W}$ represents the user latent factors, and $\mathbf{H}$ represents the item latent factors. The non-negativity constraint ensures that the components are additive, making the results easier to interpret.

Sparse coding is another technique that has gained traction for handling sparsity in recommender systems. Sparse coding involves representing data as a sparse combination of basis functions, where only a few basis functions are active at a time. This approach can effectively capture the underlying structure of the data while dealing with sparsity. The objective is to find a sparse representation $\mathbf{Z}$ such that:

$$\mathbf{X} \approx \mathbf{DZ}$$

where $\mathbf{X}$ is the original data matrix, $\mathbf{D}$ is the dictionary matrix, and $\mathbf{Z}$ is the sparse representation. The sparsity constraint ensures that each data point is represented by a combination of a small number of dictionary elements, effectively dealing with missing values.

Advanced machine learning techniques, including deep learning models, have also been employed to address sparse data in recommender systems. Deep neural networks can learn complex representations and interactions between users and items, even in the presence of sparsity. Autoencoders, a type of neural network used for unsupervised learning, can be particularly effective. Autoencoders learn to encode the input data into a lower-dimensional representation and then decode it back to the original form, effectively capturing the essential features and filling in the missing values:

$$\mathbf{h} = f(\mathbf{Wx} + \mathbf{b})$$

$$\mathbf{x}' = g(\mathbf{W}'\mathbf{h} + \mathbf{b}')$$

where $\mathbf{x}$ is the input, $\mathbf{h}$ is the hidden representation, $\mathbf{W}$ and $\mathbf{W}'$ are the weight matrices, $\mathbf{b}$ and $\mathbf{b}'$ are the bias vectors, and f and g are activation functions. By training the autoencoder to minimize the reconstruction error, the model learns to generate a complete representation of the sparse data.

The implications of effectively handling sparse data are significant for the performance and reliability of recommender systems. Properly addressing sparsity ensures that the models can accurately capture user preferences and item characteristics, leading to more relevant and personalized recommendations. Conversely, failing to handle sparse data can result in biased and unreliable models, reducing user satisfaction and engagement. Therefore, investing in robust techniques for managing sparsity is essential for the success of recommender systems.

In conclusion, handling sparse data is a critical aspect of developing effective recommender systems. Techniques such as matrix factorization, imputation methods, hybrid models, dimensionality reduction, sparse coding, and advanced machine learning approaches each contribute uniquely to addressing the challenges posed by sparse interaction matrices. By leveraging these techniques, recommender systems can generate accurate and personalized recommendations even in the presence of sparsity, enhancing user experience and engagement. As the scale and complexity of data continue to grow, innovative methods for handling sparse data will remain essential for maintaining the robustness and efficacy of recommender systems in an increasingly data-driven world.

3.6. Conclusion

The processes of data collection, cleaning, preparation, feature engineering, and handling sparse data are integral to the successful implementation of recommender systems. These stages form the foundation upon which effective and accurate recommendation models are built, each contributing uniquely to the overall robustness and reliability of the system. The preceding sections have illustrated the complexity and importance of these processes, emphasizing that the quality and comprehensiveness of the data directly influence the performance of recommender systems.

In the realm of **data collection**, the diversity and richness of the data sources—from explicit feedback like ratings and reviews to implicit feedback such as clicks and purchase history—provide a comprehensive view of user preferences. However, the abundance of data also brings challenges, including the need for sophisticated methods to integrate and harmonize data from multiple sources. Contextual information, social data, and demographic profiles further enrich the dataset, allowing for more personalized and relevant recommendations. The effective integration of these diverse data sources is crucial, requiring robust schema integration and data deduplication techniques to ensure a cohesive dataset.

The **data cleaning and preparation** phase is critical in transforming raw data into a high-quality, analyzable format. This involves addressing issues such as missing values, duplicates, and outliers, each of which can significantly distort the data analysis if not properly managed. Techniques such as imputation, normalization, and feature transformation are essential to prepare the data for modeling. Data cleaning ensures the elimination of noise and inconsistencies, while data transformation and feature engineering enhance the predictive power of the models by creating meaningful and relevant features from the raw data.

Feature engineering is particularly impactful, as it involves creating, transforming, and selecting variables that highlight the most relevant aspects of the data. Through the generation of interaction features, scaling and normalization, and encoding of categorical variables, feature engineering ensures that the models can effectively capture the underlying patterns in user preferences and item characteristics. The importance of this process cannot be overstated, as the quality of the features directly affects the model's ability to generalize and produce accurate recommendations.

The challenge of **handling sparse data** is a recurring theme in recommender systems, given the inherent sparsity of user-item interaction matrices. Techniques such as matrix factorization, imputation methods, and hybrid models are crucial in addressing this issue. Matrix factorization methods, such as SVD and ALS, decompose the interaction matrix into latent factors, uncovering hidden patterns and filling in missing values. Imputation methods provide estimates for missing interactions, while hybrid models combine various techniques to leverage their strengths and mitigate their weaknesses. Advanced machine learning approaches, including deep learning models like autoencoders, further enhance the ability to handle sparsity by learning complex representations and filling in gaps in the data.

The implications of these data processing stages are profound. High-quality data collection, cleaning, preparation, and feature engineering enable recommender systems to produce accurate, relevant, and personalized recommendations, enhancing user satisfaction and engagement. Conversely, inadequacies in these processes can lead to biased, unreliable, and untrustworthy models, undermining the system's effectiveness. The continuous refinement and innovation in these areas are essential for advancing the field of recommender systems, particularly as the volume and complexity of data continue to grow.

Moreover, the interconnectedness of these processes highlights the importance of an integrated approach to data management in recommender systems. Each stage—from data collection to handling sparse data—contributes to the overall quality of the dataset and the performance of the recommendation models. This integrated approach ensures that the data pipeline is robust, efficient, and capable of supporting sophisticated algorithms that drive the recommendations.

In conclusion, the foundational stages of data collection, cleaning, preparation, feature engineering, and handling sparse data are critical to the development of effective recommender systems. These processes ensure that the data is comprehensive, high-quality, and suitable for analysis, providing the necessary inputs for accurate and personalized recommendations. As the field continues to evolve, ongoing research and innovation in these areas will be essential to address emerging challenges and harness new opportunities, ensuring that recommender systems remain at the forefront of personalization technologies. Through meticulous attention to these foundational stages, developers can build robust, reliable, and effective recommender systems that enhance user experience and engagement in an increasingly data-driven world.

4. Collaborative Filtering Techniques

Collaborative filtering is one of the most widely used and effective techniques in recommender systems. It leverages the power of user interactions and shared preferences to predict and suggest items that users are likely to enjoy. This chapter provides a comprehensive exploration of collaborative filtering techniques, focusing on their mathematical foundations, implementation details, and practical applications. We will delve into both user-based and item-based collaborative filtering, highlighting their advantages, challenges, and real-world use cases.

4.1. User-Based Collaborative Filtering

User-based collaborative filtering (UBCF) is a seminal methodology in the realm of recommender systems, grounded in the notion that users who have demonstrated similar preferences in the past are likely to exhibit analogous preferences in the future. This method capitalizes on identifying groups of users, or "neighbors," whose past behaviors and preferences are akin to those of the target user. By leveraging the preferences of these similar users, UBCF can generate personalized recommendations, enhancing the user's overall experience. The efficacy of this approach hinges on accurately measuring the similarity between users, a task that can be approached using various statistical techniques.

The core of UBCF lies in the user-item interaction matrix, where rows represent users, columns represent items, and the entries denote user interactions such as ratings, clicks, or purchases. The primary objective is to predict the missing entries in this matrix, which correspond to items that a user has not yet interacted with but may find appealing. To determine the similarity between users, several metrics can be employed. For instance, the Pearson correlation coefficient assesses the linear relationship between two users' ratings, adjusting for differences in rating scales by considering the mean and variability of their ratings. Mathematically, the Pearson correlation between two users u and v for a set of commonly rated items I_{uv} is defined as:

$$Pearson(u, v) = \frac{\sum_{i \in I_{uv}} (r_{ui} - \bar{r_u})(r_{vi} - \bar{r_v})}{\sqrt{\sum_{i \in I_{uv}} (r_{ui} - \bar{r_u})^2} \sqrt{\sum_{i \in I_{uv}} (r_{vi} - \bar{r_v})^2}}$$

where r_{ui} and r_{vi} are the ratings of users u and v for item i, and $\bar{r_u}$ and $\bar{r_v}$ are their respective average ratings.

Alternatively, cosine similarity treats users' ratings as vectors in a multidimensional space, calculating the cosine of the angle between these vectors. This method is particularly effective when the magnitude of ratings varies widely among users, as it focuses on the direction of preferences rather than their absolute values. Cosine similarity between two users u and v can be expressed as:

$$Cosine(u, v) = \frac{\sum_{i \in I_{uv}} r_{ui} r_{vi}}{\sqrt{\sum_{i \in I_{uv}} r_{ui}^2} \sqrt{\sum_{i \in I_{uv}} r_{vi}^2}}$$

Once the similarities between users are established, the next phase involves aggregating the preferences of a target user's neighbors to predict their potential interest in unseen items. This aggregation can be accomplished through a weighted sum of the neighbors' ratings, where the weights correspond to the similarity scores. For example, if user u has not rated item i, the system can estimate this rating by considering the ratings given by similar users, weighted by their similarity to user u. The predicted rating $\hat{r}_{ui}$ can be computed as:

$$\hat{r}_{ui} = \bar{r}_u + \frac{\sum_{v \in N_u} sim(u, v)(r_{vi} - \bar{r}_v)}{\sum_{v \in N_u} |sim(u, v)|}$$

where N_u is the set of similar users to u, $sim(u, v)$ is the similarity between users u and v, and r_{vi} is the rating given by user v to item i.

While UBCF is celebrated for its ability to provide highly personalized recommendations, it is not without its challenges. One significant issue is scalability. As the number of users and items increases, the computational burden of finding similar users and aggregating their preferences escalates exponentially. This challenge is particularly acute in large-scale systems where real-time recommendation generation is necessary. Moreover, data sparsity presents another formidable obstacle. In most practical scenarios, users interact with only a small subset of available items, leading to a sparse user-item matrix. This sparsity can make it difficult to identify enough common items among users, thereby undermining the reliability of similarity measurements.

The cold start problem further complicates the application of UBCF. New users, who have limited interaction history, pose a challenge as the system lacks sufficient data to accurately identify similar users and generate recommendations. Similarly, new items, which have not been rated by many users, suffer from a lack of interaction data, making it difficult for the system to position them within the recommendation framework. Various strategies have been proposed to mitigate these issues, such as hybrid recommender systems that combine collaborative filtering with content-based methods, thereby leveraging item attributes to supplement sparse user interaction data.

In practical applications, UBCF has been successfully employed across diverse domains to enhance user engagement and satisfaction. E-commerce platforms like Amazon use UBCF to recommend products based on the purchase histories and browsing patterns of similar customers. For instance, if a user frequently buys books on a specific topic, the system can suggest additional titles favored by users with comparable interests. Streaming services, such as Netflix and Spotify, utilize UBCF to recommend movies, TV shows, and music tracks by analyzing the viewing or listening habits of users with similar tastes. This personalized content recommendation enhances user satisfaction and retention.

Social media platforms further illustrate the versatility of UBCF by using it to recommend friends, pages, groups, and content. By examining the interactions and connections of similar users, these platforms can suggest relevant connections and content, fostering a more engaging and interconnected user experience. For example, Facebook might recommend new friends based on mutual friends and shared interests, thereby enhancing the platform's social connectivity.

To address the inherent limitations of UBCF, several enhancements and variations have been developed. Hybrid systems, which integrate UBCF with other recommendation techniques such as content-based filtering and matrix factorization, offer a robust solution by leveraging the strengths of multiple approaches. For instance, a hybrid system might use content-based filtering to provide initial recommendations for new users, gradually incorporating collaborative filtering as more interaction data becomes available. Clustering techniques can also enhance UBCF by segmenting users into groups based on their preferences, reducing computational complexity and improving scalability. Within each cluster, recommendations can be generated more efficiently, ensuring that users receive timely and relevant suggestions.

Dimensionality reduction methods, such as Singular Value Decomposition (SVD) and Principal Component Analysis (PCA), can further improve UBCF by capturing the most significant patterns in the user-item interaction matrix while reducing noise. These techniques transform the high-dimensional data into a lower-dimensional space, where the key relationships between users and items are more apparent, leading to more accurate and computationally efficient recommendations.

In summary, user-based collaborative filtering remains a cornerstone of recommendation system methodologies, offering a powerful and intuitive means of generating personalized suggestions by leveraging the collective preferences of similar users. Despite its challenges, such as scalability, data sparsity, and the cold start problem, UBCF continues to be a vital tool in the development of effective recommendation systems. By understanding its underlying principles, practical applications, and potential enhancements, developers can harness the full potential of UBCF to create engaging and personalized user experiences. Through continuous refinement and the integration of complementary techniques, UBCF can be adapted to meet the evolving demands of modern recommendation systems, ensuring its relevance and effectiveness in an increasingly data-driven world.

4.2. Item-Based Collaborative Filtering

Item-based collaborative filtering (IBCF) is a prominent technique within the domain of recommender systems, distinguished by its focus on identifying similarities between items rather than users. This method operates on the principle that users are likely to show a preference for items similar to those they have previously interacted with. By leveraging item similarities, IBCF can generate personalized recommendations that enhance user experience and satisfaction. Understanding the intricacies of IBCF involves delving into its mechanisms, mathematical foundations, advantages, and practical applications, while addressing common challenges and potential solutions.

At the heart of item-based collaborative filtering is the user-item interaction matrix, where rows represent users, columns represent items, and the entries capture user interactions such as ratings, clicks, or purchases. The primary objective is to predict a user's interest in items they have not yet engaged with by examining the similarities between items they have already interacted with and those they have not. To compute the similarity between items, various metrics are employed, with cosine similarity and Pearson correlation coefficient being the most commonly used.

Cosine similarity measures the cosine of the angle between two item vectors in a multidimensional space. It is particularly useful when the magnitude of ratings varies widely among users, as it focuses on the direction of preferences rather than their absolute values. Mathematically, the cosine similarity between two items i and j is given by:

$$Cosine(i,j) = \frac{\sum_{u \in U_{ij}} r_{ui} r_{uj}}{\sqrt{\sum_{u \in U_{ij}} r_{ui}^2} \sqrt{\sum_{u \in U_{ij}} r_{uj}^2}}$$

where r_{ui} and r_{uj} are the ratings of user u for items i and j, and U_{ij} is the set of users who have rated both items.

Alternatively, the Pearson correlation coefficient assesses the linear relationship between the ratings of two items, adjusting for the mean and variability of user ratings. This measure helps to account for individual differences in rating scales. The Pearson correlation between two items i and j is defined as:

$$Pearson(i,j) = \frac{\sum_{u \in U_{ij}} (r_{ui} - \bar{r_i})(r_{uj} - \bar{r_j})}{\sqrt{\sum_{u \in U_{ij}} (r_{ui} - \bar{r_i})^2} \sqrt{\sum_{u \in U_{ij}} (r_{uj} - \bar{r_j})^2}}$$

where $\bar{r_i}$ and $\bar{r_j}$ are the average ratings of items i and j, respectively.

Once the item similarities are established, the next step in IBCF involves generating recommendations by predicting a user's rating or preference for items they have not yet interacted with. This can be achieved through a weighted sum of ratings from similar items. The predicted rating $\hat{r}_{ui}$ for a user u and an item i is computed as:

$$\hat{r}_{ui} = \frac{\sum_{j \in S(i)} sim(i,j) r_{uj}}{\sum_{j \in S(i)} |sim(i,j)|}$$

where $S(i)$ is the set of items similar to i, $sim(i,j)$ is the similarity between items i and j, and r_{uj} is the rating given by user u to item j. This approach ensures that the influence of each similar item is proportional to its similarity to the target item.

Despite its effectiveness, IBCF faces several challenges, particularly concerning the cold start problem and the computational cost of similarity calculations. The cold start problem arises when new items are introduced into the system with little to no interaction data. In such cases, it becomes difficult to accurately determine item similarities, which are crucial for generating reliable recommendations. Similarly, new users who have interacted with only a few items pose a challenge, as the system lacks sufficient data to identify items similar to those the user might prefer.

Addressing the cold start problem often involves integrating content-based filtering techniques, which utilize item attributes such as genre, price, and description to infer similarities. For example, in a movie recommendation system, content-based attributes like genre and director can be used to suggest new movies that align with a user's preferences. This hybrid approach leverages the strengths of both collaborative and content-based filtering, providing more comprehensive and accurate recommendations.

The computational cost of calculating item similarities can also be significant, especially in systems with a large number of items. To mitigate this, clustering techniques can be employed to group similar items together, reducing the complexity of similarity calculations. By clustering items into segments based on their attributes or interaction patterns, recommendations can be generated more efficiently within each cluster. This approach not only improves scalability but also enhances the relevance of recommendations by ensuring that users are presented with items from their preferred clusters.

In practical applications, IBCF has been widely adopted across various industries to enhance user engagement and satisfaction. E-commerce platforms such as Amazon utilize IBCF to recommend products that are similar to those a user has viewed or purchased. For instance, Amazon's "Customers who bought this item also bought" feature leverages item similarities to suggest related products, thereby increasing the likelihood of additional purchases.

Streaming services like Netflix and Spotify employ IBCF to recommend movies, TV shows, and music tracks. By analyzing the viewing or listening habits of users and identifying similar content, these platforms can provide personalized recommendations that enhance user retention and satisfaction. For example, if a user enjoys a particular TV series, Netflix might recommend other series with similar themes, genres, or production styles, based on the viewing patterns of users with similar tastes.

Online retail platforms also benefit from IBCF by suggesting complementary products that enhance the user's shopping experience. For instance, a fashion retailer might recommend accessories or clothing items that complement the user's current selections, thereby encouraging additional purchases and improving overall customer satisfaction.

To further enhance the performance of IBCF, advanced techniques such as matrix factorization can be employed. Matrix factorization methods, such as Singular Value Decomposition (SVD) and Alternating Least Squares (ALS), decompose the user-item interaction matrix into latent factors that capture the underlying structure of the data. These latent factors represent the intrinsic properties of users and items, enabling more accurate prediction of user preferences. By incorporating matrix factorization, IBCF can better handle data sparsity and improve the quality of recommendations.

Moreover, context-aware recommendation systems can augment IBCF by incorporating contextual information such as time, location, and user behavior. For example, a restaurant recommendation app might suggest dining options based on the user's current location and the time of day, providing more relevant and timely recommendations. This context-aware approach enhances the personalization of recommendations, further increasing user satisfaction and engagement.

In conclusion, item-based collaborative filtering is a robust and versatile technique for generating personalized recommendations by leveraging item similarities. Despite its challenges, such as the cold start problem and computational complexity, IBCF remains a vital tool in the development of effective recommender systems. By understanding its underlying principles, practical applications, and potential enhancements, developers can harness the full potential of IBCF to create engaging and personalized user experiences. Through continuous refinement and the integration of complementary techniques, IBCF can be adapted to meet the evolving demands of modern recommendation systems, ensuring its relevance and effectiveness in an increasingly data-driven world.

4.3. Real-World Applications

Recommender systems have become integral to a myriad of industries, demonstrating their value through enhanced user experiences, increased engagement, and significant business growth. These systems leverage advanced algorithms to personalize content, products, and services, thus meeting the specific needs and preferences of individual users. The real-world applications of recommender systems span across e-commerce, streaming services, social media, and beyond, each presenting unique challenges and benefits that underscore the versatility and effectiveness of these systems.

In the realm of e-commerce, recommender systems are pivotal in driving sales and improving customer satisfaction. Platforms like Amazon and Alibaba employ sophisticated recommendation algorithms to suggest products that align with a user's browsing and purchasing history. For instance, if a user frequently purchases electronic gadgets, the system might recommend the latest models or accessories that complement previous purchases. This is typically achieved through collaborative filtering techniques, which analyze the purchasing patterns of similar users to generate personalized suggestions. The mathematical foundation of these recommendations often involves similarity measures such as cosine similarity or Pearson correlation, which help identify users with comparable interests. By personalizing the shopping experience, these systems not only enhance user satisfaction but also boost sales and customer loyalty.

Streaming services like Netflix, Spotify, and YouTube have also significantly benefited from the implementation of recommender systems. These platforms utilize a combination of collaborative filtering, content-based filtering, and hybrid approaches to tailor content recommendations to individual users. For example, Netflix employs a sophisticated recommendation engine that analyzes viewing habits, genre preferences, and even the time spent watching specific types of content. This enables the platform to suggest movies and TV shows that align closely with the user's tastes. A notable application of matrix factorization techniques, such as Singular Value Decomposition (SVD), helps uncover latent factors that represent underlying patterns in user preferences, thereby improving the accuracy of recommendations. Similarly, Spotify uses collaborative filtering and deep learning models to analyze listening patterns and recommend songs and artists that users are likely to enjoy. These personalized recommendations play a crucial role in user retention, as they help users discover new content that resonates with their preferences.

Social media platforms like Facebook, Twitter, and LinkedIn leverage recommender systems to enhance user engagement and connectivity. These systems analyze user interactions, social connections, and content preferences to suggest friends, pages, groups, and posts that are likely to be of interest. For example, Facebook's friend recommendation system uses graph-based algorithms to identify potential connections by examining mutual friends and shared interests. This not only fosters a more interconnected user community but also increases the time users spend on the platform, thereby boosting engagement. LinkedIn, on the other hand, employs recommendation algorithms to suggest jobs, articles, and professional connections based on a user's profile, skills, and career aspirations. By providing relevant and timely suggestions, these platforms enhance the user experience and maintain user engagement.

Beyond these well-known applications, recommender systems are also making significant inroads in other sectors such as healthcare, education, and finance. In healthcare, personalized recommendations can assist patients in finding relevant health information, medications, and treatment options based on their medical history and current health conditions. For instance, a health platform might recommend lifestyle changes, diet plans, or exercise routines tailored to a user's specific health goals and conditions. This is achieved by analyzing user data and comparing it with large datasets of similar patients, ensuring that recommendations are both relevant and effective.

In the educational sector, recommender systems can personalize learning experiences by suggesting courses, reading materials, and learning paths that match a student's interests and academic goals. Platforms like Coursera and Khan Academy utilize these systems to recommend courses based on a student's past performance, interests, and learning pace. By providing personalized learning recommendations, these platforms enhance the educational experience and support students in achieving their academic objectives.

The finance industry also benefits from recommender systems through personalized financial advice, investment recommendations, and fraud detection. Financial platforms use these systems to analyze user transactions, investment patterns, and financial goals to suggest investment opportunities, savings plans, and budgeting advice. For example, a financial app might recommend specific stocks or mutual funds based on a user's risk tolerance and investment history. Additionally, recommender systems can play a crucial role in detecting fraudulent activities by identifying unusual transaction patterns and alerting users to potential security threats.

Despite their widespread adoption and success, recommender systems are not without challenges. Issues such as data sparsity, scalability, and the cold start problem remain significant obstacles that developers must address. Data sparsity, where users interact with only a small fraction of available items, can undermine the accuracy of recommendations. Scalability challenges arise as the number of users and items grows, increasing the computational demands of generating real-time recommendations. The cold start problem, involving new users or items with insufficient interaction data, makes it difficult to provide accurate recommendations initially.

To overcome these challenges, advancements in machine learning and artificial intelligence continue to play a pivotal role. Techniques such as deep learning, reinforcement learning, and hybrid models are increasingly being employed to enhance the accuracy, efficiency, and scalability of recommender systems. For example, deep learning models can capture complex patterns and relationships in large datasets, providing more nuanced and accurate recommendations. Reinforcement learning, which treats the recommendation process as a sequential decision-making problem, can optimize long-term user engagement by continuously learning and adapting to user preferences.

In conclusion, the real-world applications of recommender systems are vast and varied, spanning multiple industries and significantly enhancing user experiences and business outcomes. By leveraging advanced algorithms and machine learning techniques, these systems provide personalized recommendations that cater to individual preferences, thereby driving engagement, satisfaction, and loyalty. Despite the challenges, ongoing advancements in technology continue to improve the effectiveness and efficiency of recommender systems, ensuring their continued relevance and impact in an increasingly data-driven world. Through thoughtful implementation and continuous refinement, recommender systems will remain a cornerstone of personalized user experiences across diverse domains.

4.4. Conclusion

Collaborative filtering techniques have cemented their position as fundamental methodologies in the field of recommender systems, due to their ability to leverage the collective intelligence embedded in user-item interactions. These techniques, which include both user-based and item-based collaborative filtering, harness the patterns and preferences demonstrated by users to generate personalized recommendations. Their widespread adoption across various industries, from e-commerce and streaming services to social media and beyond, underscores their versatility and efficacy. Understanding the underlying principles, mathematical foundations, and practical applications of collaborative filtering is essential for developing sophisticated and effective recommendation systems.

User-based collaborative filtering (UBCF) operates on the premise that users with similar preferences in the past will continue to exhibit similar preferences in the future. By identifying a target user's nearest neighbors—those users whose past behaviors align closely with the target user's behaviors—UBCF can provide highly personalized recommendations. The similarity between users is often quantified using statistical measures such as the Pearson correlation coefficient and cosine similarity. For instance, the Pearson correlation coefficient accounts for individual differences in rating scales by considering the mean and variability of users' ratings, thereby providing a robust measure of linear relationship between users. In practice, this approach has been effectively utilized by platforms like Amazon and Netflix to recommend products and content based on the preferences of users with similar tastes.

Conversely, item-based collaborative filtering (IBCF) shifts the focus from users to items, identifying similarities between items rather than users. This method is particularly advantageous in scenarios where the number of items is significantly smaller and more stable compared to the number of users, thereby enhancing scalability. Similarity between items can be measured using metrics such as cosine similarity and Pearson correlation coefficient, which help in identifying items frequently rated or interacted with similarly by users. By leveraging these item similarities, IBCF generates recommendations by predicting a user's interest in items they have not yet interacted with, based on their past interactions with similar items. This approach has been successfully implemented by streaming services like Spotify and Netflix, which use IBCF to recommend music tracks and movies that align with users' listening and viewing histories.

Both UBCF and IBCF face certain challenges that necessitate ongoing refinement and innovation. One significant issue is data sparsity, which occurs when users interact with only a small fraction of available items, resulting in a sparse user-item interaction matrix. This sparsity can undermine the reliability of similarity measurements and hinder the accuracy of recommendations. Additionally, the cold start problem presents a formidable challenge, particularly for new users and items with insufficient interaction data. To mitigate these issues, hybrid recommender systems have been developed, combining collaborative filtering with content-based methods to leverage item attributes and supplement sparse user interaction data. For instance, a hybrid system might use content-based filtering to provide initial recommendations for new users, gradually incorporating collaborative filtering as more interaction data becomes available.

Advancements in machine learning and artificial intelligence have further enhanced the effectiveness of collaborative filtering techniques. Matrix factorization methods, such as Singular Value Decomposition (SVD) and Alternating Least Squares (ALS), decompose the user-item interaction matrix into latent factors that capture the underlying structure of the data. These latent factors represent intrinsic properties of users and items, enabling more accurate prediction of user preferences. For example, SVD helps uncover latent patterns in the data, improving the accuracy of recommendations by predicting missing entries in the user-item matrix. Similarly, deep learning models, which can capture complex patterns and relationships in large datasets, are increasingly being employed to enhance the accuracy and efficiency of collaborative filtering.

In real-world applications, collaborative filtering techniques have demonstrated their value through significant business outcomes and enhanced user experiences. E-commerce platforms use these techniques to drive sales by recommending products that align with users' browsing and purchasing histories. Streaming services employ collaborative filtering to suggest movies, TV shows, and music tracks that resonate with users' tastes, thereby improving user retention and satisfaction. Social media platforms leverage these techniques to enhance user engagement by recommending friends, pages, groups, and content based on users' interactions and connections.

The success of collaborative filtering techniques lies in their ability to personalize the user experience by leveraging collective intelligence. By analyzing user-item interactions and identifying patterns and similarities, these techniques can provide tailored recommendations that meet the specific needs and preferences of individual users. This personalized approach not only enhances user satisfaction but also drives engagement and loyalty, resulting in significant business benefits.

Despite the challenges, the continued evolution of collaborative filtering techniques promises to address their limitations and enhance their effectiveness. The integration of advanced machine learning models, the development of hybrid systems, and the incorporation of contextual information are among the strategies that hold the potential to further improve the accuracy, scalability, and robustness of collaborative filtering. As the field of recommender systems continues to evolve, collaborative filtering techniques will remain a cornerstone, providing the foundation for personalized user experiences across diverse domains.

In conclusion, collaborative filtering techniques are indispensable in the landscape of recommender systems, offering powerful tools for generating personalized recommendations. Their application across various industries highlights their versatility and impact, while ongoing advancements in technology continue to enhance their capabilities. By understanding the principles, challenges, and practical applications of user-based and item-based collaborative filtering, developers can harness the full potential of these techniques to create sophisticated and effective recommendation systems. Through continuous innovation and refinement, collaborative filtering will continue to play a crucial role in shaping personalized user experiences in an increasingly data-driven world.

5. Content-Based Filtering Methods

Content-based filtering represents a powerful approach in the realm of recommender systems, focusing on the intrinsic attributes of items to generate personalized recommendations. Unlike collaborative filtering, which relies on user interaction data, content-based filtering leverages the features of items and the preferences of users to make recommendations. This chapter delves into the principles of content-based filtering, detailing how to extract and represent item features, measure similarity, and implement effective content-based recommendation models.

5.1. Principles of Content-Based Filtering

Content-based filtering is a robust and widely utilized technique in the domain of recommender systems, distinguished by its reliance on the intrinsic attributes of items to generate recommendations. Unlike collaborative filtering, which leverages user-item interaction patterns to find similarities among users or items, content-based filtering operates by analyzing the features of items and aligning them with user preferences. This method offers several advantages, particularly in terms of addressing the cold start problem and providing transparent, explainable recommendations. Understanding the principles of content-based filtering requires a deep dive into its theoretical foundations, practical applications, and the mathematical frameworks that underpin its functionality.

At the core of content-based filtering is the representation of items through a set of features or attributes. These features can vary widely depending on the domain. For instance, in a movie recommendation system, relevant features might include genre, director, cast, and keywords extracted from the movie's synopsis. Similarly, in a book recommendation system, features could encompass genre, author, publication date, and thematic keywords. These features are typically represented as vectors in a multidimensional space, enabling the comparison of items based on their attributes.

A fundamental step in content-based filtering is the construction of user profiles. These profiles encapsulate the preferences of users by aggregating the features of items they have previously interacted with. For instance, if a user has rated several action movies highly, their profile might emphasize the action genre and related attributes such as specific directors or actors. This user profile serves as a reference point for generating recommendations, as it is used to identify items with similar features that the user has not yet encountered.

Mathematically, the process of matching items to user profiles often involves calculating the similarity between the item feature vectors and the user profile vector. One common similarity measure used in this context is cosine similarity, which quantifies the cosine of the angle between two vectors. Given an item vector $\mathbf{v_i}$ and a user profile vector $\mathbf{u}$, the cosine similarity $\text{sim}(\mathbf{u}, \mathbf{v_i})$ is defined as:

$$sim(\mathbf{u}, \mathbf{v_i}) = \frac{\mathbf{u} \cdot \mathbf{v_i}}{\| \mathbf{u} \| \| \mathbf{v_i} \|} = \frac{\sum_{k=1}^{n} u_k v_{i,k}}{\sqrt{\sum_{k=1}^{n} u_k^2}\sqrt{\sum_{k=1}^{n} v_{i,k}^2}}$$

where $\mathbf{u} \cdot \mathbf{v_i}$ denotes the dot product of the user profile and item vectors, and $\| \mathbf{u} \|$ and $\| \mathbf{v_i} \|$ represent their Euclidean norms. This measure provides a normalized similarity score ranging from -1 to 1, with higher values indicating greater similarity.

The practical implementation of content-based filtering can be observed in various applications. For instance, news recommendation systems like those used by Google News analyze the content of articles, including the headline, body text, and keywords, to recommend news stories that align with the user's reading history and stated interests. If a user frequently reads articles on technology and startups, the system will prioritize recommending similar content, ensuring that the recommendations are relevant and tailored to the user's preferences.

Similarly, in the domain of music streaming, platforms like Spotify employ content-based filtering to suggest songs and artists based on the attributes of tracks the user has previously enjoyed. These attributes might include genre, tempo, instrumentation, and lyrical themes. By constructing a detailed profile of the user's musical tastes, the system can recommend new tracks that share similar characteristics, enhancing the user's discovery experience and satisfaction.

One of the key advantages of content-based filtering is its ability to address the cold start problem, particularly for new items. Since the recommendations are based on the attributes of the items rather than user interactions, new items with detailed attribute information can be recommended immediately. For example, a newly released book can be recommended to users whose profiles indicate a preference for similar genres or themes, even if the book has not yet garnered many user ratings or reviews. This capability ensures that content-based systems can provide timely and relevant recommendations for fresh content.

Another significant benefit of content-based filtering is the transparency and explainability of its recommendations. Because the recommendations are derived from the explicit attributes of items, it is straightforward to articulate why a particular item was recommended. For instance, a movie recommendation system might explain that a user is being recommended a film because it shares the same genre and lead actor as other movies the user has rated highly. This transparency can enhance user trust and satisfaction, as users can clearly understand the rationale behind the recommendations.

Despite its advantages, content-based filtering is not without its challenges. One notable limitation is the potential for over-specialization, where the system repeatedly recommends items that are too similar to those the user has already encountered, limiting the diversity of recommendations. This issue arises because the system

54

focuses solely on matching item attributes to the user profile, potentially overlooking novel or diverse content that might still be of interest to the user. To mitigate this, hybrid recommender systems often integrate content-based filtering with collaborative filtering techniques, balancing the precision of content-based recommendations with the serendipity and diversity provided by collaborative approaches.

Additionally, the effectiveness of content-based filtering is heavily dependent on the quality and richness of the item features. In domains where item attributes are not well-defined or difficult to extract, the performance of content-based systems can suffer. Advanced techniques such as natural language processing (NLP) and machine learning are often employed to extract meaningful features from unstructured data, such as text, images, and audio. For instance, NLP techniques can be used to analyze and categorize the themes and sentiments in user reviews or article content, enriching the feature set available for recommendation.

In conclusion, content-based filtering is a powerful and flexible approach to generating personalized recommendations by leveraging the inherent attributes of items. Its ability to provide transparent, explainable recommendations and address the cold start problem makes it a valuable tool in various applications, from news and music recommendation to e-commerce and beyond. However, to fully realize its potential, it is essential to address challenges related to over-specialization and feature extraction. By integrating content-based filtering with other recommendation techniques and employing advanced data processing methods, developers can enhance the accuracy, diversity, and relevance of recommendations, ultimately improving user satisfaction and engagement. Through a deep understanding of its principles and practical applications, content-based filtering will continue to play a crucial role in the development of sophisticated recommender systems in an increasingly data-driven world.

5.2. Feature Extraction and Representation

Feature extraction and representation lie at the heart of content-based filtering systems, forming the foundation upon which accurate and relevant recommendations are built. The process involves identifying, extracting, and representing the essential characteristics or attributes of items in a manner that allows the recommendation algorithm to effectively compare and contrast these items against user preferences. The success of content-based filtering depends significantly on the quality and richness of the features extracted from the items, as these features directly influence the system's ability to discern similarities and differences among items.

The initial step in feature extraction is to determine the relevant attributes that characterize each item within the domain. These attributes, often referred to as features, can vary widely depending on the nature of the items being recommended. For instance, in a movie recommendation system, features might include genre, director, cast, release year, and keywords extracted from the plot summary. In a music recommendation system, features could encompass genre, artist, tempo, key, and lyrical themes. The identification of these features is crucial as it directly impacts the system's ability to generate meaningful recommendations.

Once the relevant features have been identified, the next step involves extracting these features from the raw data. This process can be straightforward or complex depending on the type and structure of the data. For structured data, such as tabular datasets with clearly defined columns for each attribute, feature extraction can be relatively simple. However, for unstructured data, such as text, images, or audio, more sophisticated techniques are required to extract meaningful features. For example, in text-based data, natural language processing (NLP) techniques such as tokenization, stemming, lemmatization, and named entity recognition (NER) are commonly employed to process and extract relevant keywords and phrases from documents.

A critical aspect of feature extraction is the representation of these features in a form that can be effectively utilized by the recommendation algorithm. This often involves transforming the raw features into numerical vectors that capture the essence of the items. In text-based applications, techniques such as Term Frequency-Inverse Document Frequency (TF-IDF) and word embeddings (e.g., Word2Vec, GloVe) are used to convert text into numerical vectors. TF-IDF, for instance, measures the importance of a term within a document relative to its occurrence in a corpus, providing a weighted representation that reflects the significance of each term. Mathematically, the TF-IDF score for a term t in a document d is calculated as:

$$TF\text{-}IDF(t, d) = TF(t, d) \times IDF(t)$$

where $TF(t, d)$ is the term frequency of t in d, and $IDF(t)$ is the inverse document frequency of t across the corpus. The term frequency is the number of times t appears in d, and the inverse document frequency is given by:

$$IDF(t) = \log\left(\frac{N}{1 + |\{d : t \in d\}|}\right)$$

where N is the total number of documents in the corpus, and $|\{d : t \in d\}|$ is the number of documents containing t.

Word embeddings, on the other hand, provide dense vector representations of words by training models on large text corpora to capture semantic similarities and relationships between words. For example, Word2Vec uses a neural network to learn word vectors that place semantically similar words close to each other in the vector space, enabling the recommendation system to understand and utilize the contextual meaning of words.

For numerical and categorical features, various scaling and encoding techniques are applied to ensure that the features are represented on a comparable scale and format. Min-max scaling, for instance, transforms numerical features to a specified range, typically [0, 1], preserving the relationships between data points while standardizing the scale. Categorical features can be encoded using methods such as one-hot encoding, which converts categorical values into binary vectors, or label encoding, which assigns a unique integer to each category. These transformations are essential for ensuring that the features contribute equitably to the recommendation process.

The effectiveness of feature extraction and representation is not only contingent on the selection and transformation of individual features but also on the ability to capture interactions and relationships between features. Techniques such as polynomial feature generation and interaction terms can be employed to create new features that represent the combined effect of multiple attributes. For example, in a movie recommendation system, an interaction term between the genre and the lead actor could capture the unique appeal of specific actor-genre combinations, enhancing the system's ability to provide nuanced recommendations.

Advanced machine learning models, such as deep learning networks, offer powerful tools for automatic feature extraction and representation. Convolutional neural networks (CNNs) and recurrent neural networks (RNNs), for instance, have been successfully applied to image and text data, respectively, to extract high-level features that capture complex patterns and structures. CNNs, with their ability to learn spatial hierarchies, are particularly effective in processing image data, identifying salient features such as shapes, textures, and objects. RNNs, with their capability to handle sequential data, excel in tasks involving text and time-series data, capturing temporal dependencies and contextual relationships.

In practical applications, feature extraction and representation play a pivotal role in the success of content-based recommendation systems. For instance, news recommendation systems like those used by Google News rely on sophisticated NLP techniques to extract and represent features from article content, enabling the system to recommend news stories that align with users' reading preferences. Similarly, e-commerce platforms such as Amazon use a combination of structured and unstructured data to extract features from product descriptions, reviews, and specifications, providing personalized product recommendations that cater to individual user preferences.

The implications of effective feature extraction and representation extend beyond improved recommendation accuracy. They also contribute to the interpretability and transparency of the recommendation process. By clearly defining and representing the features that drive recommendations, content-based systems can provide explanations that help users understand why certain items are being suggested. This transparency fosters user trust and satisfaction, as users can see the rationale behind the recommendations and feel more confident in the system's ability to meet their needs.

In conclusion, feature extraction and representation are fundamental to the efficacy of content-based filtering systems. The process involves identifying relevant attributes, extracting meaningful features from raw data, and transforming these features into numerical vectors that accurately capture the essence of the items. By leveraging advanced techniques such as NLP, word embeddings, scaling, encoding, and deep learning, developers can enhance the quality and richness of the features, thereby improving the accuracy, diversity, and relevance of recommendations. Through meticulous feature extraction and representation, content-based filtering systems can provide personalized and transparent recommendations that cater to the unique preferences of individual users, ultimately driving user engagement and satisfaction in an increasingly data-driven world.

5.3. Similarity Measures

Similarity measures are a cornerstone in the realm of content-based filtering, playing a pivotal role in determining how closely related items are to each other and to user preferences. The essence of content-based filtering lies in comparing items based on their attributes and identifying those that align most closely with a user's tastes. This comparison hinges on robust and accurate similarity measures, which quantify the degree of likeness between items or between items and user profiles. Understanding these measures involves delving into their mathematical foundations, practical applications, and the implications of their use in real-world recommender systems.

At the heart of similarity measurement in content-based filtering is the concept of vector space representation. Items are represented as vectors in a multidimensional space, where each dimension corresponds to a specific feature of the items. This representation allows for the application of various mathematical techniques to compute the similarity between items. One of the most widely used similarity measures in this context is cosine similarity. Cosine similarity measures the cosine of the angle between two vectors, effectively capturing the orientation of the vectors in the feature space rather than their magnitude. This property makes it particularly useful when the magnitude of the feature values varies widely among items. The cosine similarity between two item vectors $\mathbf{v_i}$ and $\mathbf{v_j}$ is defined as:

$$cosine(\mathbf{v_i}, \mathbf{v_j}) = \frac{\mathbf{v_i} \cdot \mathbf{v_j}}{\| \mathbf{v_i} \| \| \mathbf{v_j} \|} = \frac{\sum_{k=1}^{n} v_{i,k} v_{j,k}}{\sqrt{\sum_{k=1}^{n} v_{i,k}^2} \sqrt{\sum_{k=1}^{n} v_{j,k}^2}}$$

where $\mathbf{v_i} \cdot \mathbf{v_j}$ denotes the dot product of the vectors, and $\| \mathbf{v_i} \|$ and $\| \mathbf{v_j} \|$ represent their Euclidean norms. A cosine similarity score close to 1 indicates that the items are very similar, while a score close to 0 indicates little to no similarity.

Another important similarity measure is the Pearson correlation coefficient, which assesses the linear relationship between the ratings or feature values of two items. The

58

Pearson correlation takes into account the mean and variability of the ratings, providing a normalized measure of similarity that is robust to differences in rating scales. The Pearson correlation between two items i and j is given by:

$$Pearson(i,j) = \frac{\sum_{u \in U_{ij}} (r_{ui} - \bar{r_i})(r_{uj} - \bar{r_j})}{\sqrt{\sum_{u \in U_{ij}} (r_{ui} - \bar{r_i})^2} \sqrt{\sum_{u \in U_{ij}} (r_{uj} - \bar{r_j})^2}}$$

where r_{ui} and r_{uj} are the ratings given by user u to items i and j respectively, $\bar{r_i}$ and $\bar{r_j}$ are the average ratings of items i and j, and U_{ij} is the set of users who have rated both items. This measure provides insight into the degree to which users agree on their evaluations of the items, making it particularly useful in collaborative filtering scenarios.

Euclidean distance is another measure used to determine similarity, especially in contexts where the absolute differences between feature values are meaningful. The Euclidean distance between two vectors $\mathbf{v_i}$ and $\mathbf{v_j}$ is calculated as:

$$Euclidean(\mathbf{v_i}, \mathbf{v_j}) = \sqrt{\sum_{k=1}^{n} (v_{i,k} - v_{j,k})^2}$$

This measure directly computes the geometric distance between the points in the feature space, with smaller distances indicating higher similarity. However, Euclidean distance can be sensitive to the scale of the features, necessitating the use of normalization techniques to ensure fair comparisons.

The choice of similarity measure can significantly impact the performance and behavior of a content-based recommendation system. Each measure has its strengths and limitations, and the appropriateness of a measure depends on the specific characteristics of the data and the application domain. For instance, cosine similarity is advantageous in scenarios where the direction of the feature vectors is more important than their magnitude, such as in text-based applications where term frequencies can vary widely. Pearson correlation is particularly useful when dealing with user ratings, as it normalizes for different rating scales and focuses on the linear relationship between ratings.

In practical applications, these similarity measures are employed to identify items that are most relevant to a user's profile. For example, in a movie recommendation system, cosine similarity can be used to compare the feature vectors of movies based on attributes such as genre, director, and cast. If a user has shown a preference for action movies directed by a particular director, the system can use cosine similarity to identify other movies with similar attributes and recommend them to the user. Similarly, in a music recommendation system, Pearson correlation can be used to compare the ratings of songs by different users, helping to identify songs that are likely to be enjoyed by users with similar musical tastes.

The implications of using similarity measures extend beyond the accuracy of recommendations. They also influence the diversity and novelty of the recommendations. For instance, measures that heavily rely on feature overlap, such as cosine similarity, may result in recommendations that are too similar to what the user has already experienced, potentially limiting the exposure to new and diverse content. To address this, hybrid approaches that combine multiple similarity measures or integrate collaborative filtering techniques can be employed to balance precision with diversity.

Advanced machine learning techniques can further enhance the computation and application of similarity measures. For example, deep learning models can learn complex, non-linear relationships between features, providing more nuanced and accurate similarity assessments. Techniques such as neural collaborative filtering, which integrates neural networks with traditional collaborative filtering, leverage the power of deep learning to capture intricate patterns in user-item interactions, improving the quality of recommendations.

In conclusion, similarity measures are fundamental to the effectiveness of content-based filtering systems, providing the means to compare items and align them with user preferences. By understanding and appropriately applying measures such as cosine similarity, Pearson correlation, and Euclidean distance, developers can enhance the accuracy and relevance of recommendations. The choice of similarity measure should be guided by the specific characteristics of the data and the goals of the recommendation system. Through careful selection and implementation of these measures, content-based filtering systems can deliver personalized and engaging user experiences, driving satisfaction and loyalty in a variety of applications. The continuous evolution of similarity measures and their integration with advanced machine learning techniques promise to further refine and expand the capabilities of recommender systems in an increasingly complex and data-rich world.

5.4. Building User Profiles

Building user profiles is a fundamental process in content-based filtering systems, essential for delivering personalized recommendations that align closely with individual preferences. User profiles are constructed by aggregating and analyzing the characteristics of items that users have interacted with, creating a comprehensive representation of their tastes and interests. This process involves several stages, including data collection, feature extraction, and profile construction, each requiring careful consideration to ensure the accuracy and relevance of the recommendations generated.

The first step in building user profiles is the collection of interaction data, which encompasses various forms of user engagement with items. These interactions can include explicit feedback, such as ratings and reviews, as well as implicit feedback, like clicks, views, and purchases. For instance, in an e-commerce setting, a user's purchase history, browsing behavior, and product ratings collectively contribute valuable data points that reflect their preferences. Similarly, in a music streaming service, the songs a user listens to, the frequency of plays, and their ratings provide insight into their musical tastes. The richness and diversity of this interaction data form the foundation upon which user profiles are built.

Once the interaction data is collected, the next step involves feature extraction, where the relevant attributes of the interacted items are identified and represented in a structured format. This process often requires transforming raw data into meaningful features that capture the essence of the items. For text-based data, natural language processing (NLP) techniques such as tokenization, stemming, and named entity recognition (NER) are employed to extract keywords and phrases that describe the content. For instance, in a movie recommendation system, features might include genre, director, cast, and plot keywords. These features are then used to represent the items as vectors in a multidimensional space.

The core of user profile construction lies in aggregating these item features to create a composite representation of the user's preferences. This aggregation can be performed using various methods, depending on the nature of the interaction data and the recommendation algorithm. One common approach is to use a weighted average of the feature vectors of the items the user has interacted with, where the weights correspond to the strength of the interaction. For example, if a user has rated several movies highly, the feature vectors of these movies can be combined, weighted by the user's ratings, to form the user profile vector. Mathematically, the user profile vector $\mathbf{u}$ can be expressed as:

$$\mathbf{u} = \frac{\sum_{i \in I_u} w_{ui} \mathbf{v_i}}{\sum_{i \in I_u} w_{ui}}$$

where I_u is the set of items interacted with by user u, w_{ui} is the weight of the interaction (e.g., rating), and $\mathbf{v_i}$ is the feature vector of item i. This weighted aggregation ensures that items with stronger interactions (higher ratings or more frequent plays) have a greater influence on the user profile.

The resulting user profile vector encapsulates the user's preferences in terms of the attributes of the items they have interacted with. For example, in a book recommendation system, if a user frequently reads science fiction novels by specific authors, the user profile will reflect a high affinity for the science fiction genre and those authors, enabling the system to recommend similar books. This approach not only captures explicit preferences but also implicitly infers broader interests by identifying patterns in the interaction data.

One of the key implications of building user profiles is the ability to generate highly personalized recommendations. By comparing the user profile vector to the feature vectors of available items, the system can identify items that closely match the user's preferences. This comparison is often facilitated by similarity measures such as cosine similarity, which quantifies the alignment between the user profile and item vectors. The cosine similarity $sim(\mathbf{u}, \mathbf{v_i})$ between a user profile vector $\mathbf{u}$ and an item vector $\mathbf{v_i}$ is calculated as:

$$sim(\mathbf{u}, \mathbf{v_i}) = \frac{\mathbf{u} \cdot \mathbf{v_i}}{\| \mathbf{u} \| \| \mathbf{v_i} \|}$$

where $\mathbf{u} \cdot \mathbf{v_i}$ denotes the dot product, and $\| \mathbf{u} \|$ and $\| \mathbf{v_i} \|$ are the Euclidean norms of the vectors. A high similarity score indicates that the item shares many attributes with the user's preferences, making it a strong candidate for recommendation.

The process of building user profiles also involves addressing challenges related to data sparsity and the cold start problem. Data sparsity occurs when users interact with only a small fraction of available items, resulting in incomplete profiles that may not fully capture their preferences. To mitigate this, hybrid recommender systems often integrate collaborative filtering techniques, which leverage the preferences of similar users to supplement the user profile. For instance, in a movie recommendation system, the preferences of users with similar tastes can be used to enrich the profile of a user with sparse interaction data.

The cold start problem, which affects new users with limited interaction history, can be alleviated by incorporating demographic information and explicit preferences provided during the onboarding process. For example, a new user joining a music streaming service might be asked to specify their favorite genres and artists, which can be used to initialize their profile. Additionally, content-based filtering techniques that rely on item attributes can provide immediate recommendations for new items, ensuring that they are exposed to users even in the absence of extensive interaction data.

In practical applications, the construction of user profiles plays a critical role in enhancing the user experience and driving engagement. For instance, news recommendation systems like those used by Google News build user profiles based on the topics and sources users frequently read, enabling the system to recommend articles that align with their interests. Similarly, e-commerce platforms such as Amazon use user profiles to suggest products that match a user's browsing and purchasing history, improving the relevance and appeal of recommendations.

The continuous refinement and updating of user profiles are essential for maintaining their accuracy and relevance. As users interact with new items, their profiles should be dynamically updated to reflect their evolving preferences. This requires real-time processing and integration of interaction data, ensuring that the recommendations remain current and personalized. Advanced machine learning techniques, including online learning algorithms and reinforcement learning, can facilitate this dynamic updating process, enabling the system to adapt to changes in user behavior and preferences.

In conclusion, building user profiles is a fundamental aspect of content-based filtering systems, enabling the generation of personalized recommendations that closely align with individual preferences. By collecting and analyzing interaction data, extracting meaningful features, and constructing composite representations of user tastes, these profiles provide a robust foundation for recommendation algorithms. The implications of effective user profiling extend beyond improved recommendation accuracy, fostering user satisfaction and engagement across various applications. Through continuous refinement and the integration of advanced techniques, user profiles will remain a cornerstone of personalized recommender systems in an increasingly data-driven world.

5.5. Recommendation Generation

Recommendation generation is the culmination of the processes involved in building recommender systems, wherein the system leverages user profiles, item features, and similarity measures to produce personalized suggestions. This phase integrates the insights derived from feature extraction, similarity computation, and user profiling to deliver recommendations that are relevant and tailored to individual user preferences. The generation of recommendations involves sophisticated algorithms and mathematical models, ensuring that the suggestions not only align with user tastes but also contribute to enhanced user satisfaction and engagement.

At the heart of recommendation generation lies the comparison between user profiles and item features, facilitated by similarity measures. This comparison enables the system to rank items based on their relevance to the user's preferences. For instance, in a content-based recommendation system, the similarity between the user's profile vector and the feature vectors of potential items is computed using measures such as cosine similarity. The cosine similarity $sim(\mathbf{u}, \mathbf{v_i})$ between the user profile vector $\mathbf{u}$ and an item vector $\mathbf{v_i}$ is defined as:

$$sim(\mathbf{u}, \mathbf{v_i}) = \frac{\mathbf{u} \cdot \mathbf{v_i}}{\| \mathbf{u} \| \| \mathbf{v_i} \|}$$

where $\mathbf{u} \cdot \mathbf{v_i}$ denotes the dot product, and $\| \mathbf{u} \|$ and $\| \mathbf{v_i} \|$ are the Euclidean norms of the user profile and item vectors, respectively. A high similarity score indicates a strong alignment between the user's preferences and the item's attributes, making it a prime candidate for recommendation.

The generation of recommendations involves ranking items based on their similarity scores and selecting the top-N items to present to the user. This process ensures that the most relevant items are prioritized, enhancing the likelihood of user engagement. For example, in an e-commerce platform like Amazon, the system might recommend the top ten products that closely match the user's browsing history and purchase patterns. Similarly, in a music streaming service like Spotify, the top-N songs that align with the user's listening habits and genre preferences are recommended, ensuring a personalized listening experience.

An essential aspect of recommendation generation is the incorporation of contextual information, which can significantly enhance the relevance and timeliness of recommendations. Contextual information includes factors such as the user's location, time of day, device type, and current activity. By integrating this information, the system can tailor recommendations to the user's current context, thereby improving their relevance. For instance, a restaurant recommendation app might suggest nearby dining options based on the user's current location and the time of day, providing timely and contextually appropriate suggestions. Similarly, a news recommendation system might prioritize breaking news stories during the morning commute, aligning with the user's likely interest in staying updated during that time.

The effectiveness of recommendation generation is also influenced by the diversity and novelty of the suggestions. While it is crucial to recommend items that closely match the user's preferences, providing a diverse set of recommendations can enhance the user experience by exposing them to a broader range of content. This approach mitigates the risk of over-specialization, where the system repeatedly recommends items that are too similar, limiting the user's exposure to new and varied content. For example, a movie recommendation system might include a mix of genres and directors in its top-N recommendations, even if the user's profile indicates a strong preference for a particular genre. This strategy not only broadens the user's viewing options but also increases the likelihood of discovering new interests.

To achieve a balance between relevance and diversity, hybrid recommendation systems often integrate multiple algorithms and techniques. These systems combine content-based filtering with collaborative filtering and other methods, leveraging the strengths of each approach to generate comprehensive and well-rounded recommendations. For instance, a hybrid system might use collaborative filtering to identify items that are popular among similar users and content-based filtering to ensure that these items align with the user's specific preferences. This integration enhances the robustness and accuracy of the recommendations, providing a richer and more satisfying user experience.

Advanced machine learning models, including deep learning and reinforcement learning, are increasingly being employed to refine recommendation generation. Deep learning models, such as convolutional neural networks (CNNs) and recurrent neural networks (RNNs), can capture complex patterns and relationships in user behavior and item attributes, leading to more nuanced and accurate recommendations. Reinforcement learning, which treats the recommendation process as a sequential decision-making problem, can optimize long-term user engagement by continuously learning and adapting to user preferences. These advanced techniques enable the system to dynamically update recommendations in real-time, responding to changes in user behavior and context.

For instance, a streaming service might use a deep learning model to analyze the temporal patterns in a user's listening history, identifying shifts in genre preferences over time. This analysis allows the system to recommend songs that not only match the user's current preferences but also anticipate future interests based on emerging patterns. Similarly, an e-commerce platform might employ reinforcement learning to optimize the sequence of product recommendations, maximizing the likelihood of purchase by adapting to the user's interactions in real-time.

The generation of recommendations also involves addressing potential biases and ensuring fairness. Biases can arise from various sources, including historical data, algorithmic design, and user interactions. For example, if a recommendation system predominantly suggests items from a specific category due to historical popularity, it might inadvertently marginalize other categories, leading to a skewed and unbalanced recommendation set. To mitigate such biases, developers can employ techniques such as fairness-aware algorithms and diverse training datasets, ensuring that the recommendations are equitable and representative of a broad spectrum of items.

In conclusion, recommendation generation is a critical phase in content-based filtering systems, integrating user profiles, item features, similarity measures, and contextual information to deliver personalized and relevant suggestions. By leveraging advanced algorithms and machine learning models, systems can enhance the accuracy, diversity, and novelty of recommendations, ultimately driving user engagement and satisfaction. The continuous refinement and adaptation of these systems to user behavior and context ensure that recommendations remain dynamic and responsive, providing a tailored and enriching user experience in an increasingly data-driven world. Through a deep understanding of the principles and techniques involved in recommendation generation, developers can create sophisticated recommender systems that meet the evolving needs and preferences of users across various domains.

5.6. Advantages and Challenges

Content-based filtering, as a prominent technique in recommender systems, presents a host of advantages and challenges that are pivotal to its implementation and efficacy. The inherent strengths of this approach lie in its ability to generate personalized recommendations based on the explicit attributes of items, ensuring that the suggestions are directly aligned with the user's stated preferences. However, the technique is not without its drawbacks, including potential issues related to data sparsity, over-specialization, and the need for extensive feature engineering. A nuanced understanding of these advantages and challenges is essential for leveraging content-based filtering effectively.

One of the primary advantages of content-based filtering is its capacity to provide highly personalized recommendations. By analyzing the specific features of items that a user has previously interacted with, the system can tailor recommendations that closely match the user's interests. This attribute-driven approach ensures that the recommendations are grounded in the actual content characteristics that the user finds appealing. For instance, in a book recommendation system, if a user frequently reads science fiction novels, the system can recommend other science fiction titles with similar themes, authors, or narrative styles. This high degree of personalization enhances user satisfaction and engagement, as the recommendations are relevant and aligned with the user's preferences.

Another significant advantage of content-based filtering is its ability to address the cold start problem, particularly for new items. In collaborative filtering systems, the cold start problem arises because new items or users have limited interaction data, making it difficult to generate accurate recommendations. However, content-based filtering can mitigate this issue by relying on the inherent attributes of new items. For example, a newly released movie can be recommended to users whose profiles indicate a preference for similar genres or directors, even if the movie has not yet been widely rated. This capability ensures that new content can be effectively introduced to users, maintaining the dynamism and relevance of the recommendation system.

Content-based filtering also offers the advantage of transparency and explainability. Since the recommendations are based on explicit item attributes, it is relatively straightforward to articulate the rationale behind a given recommendation. For example, a music recommendation system can explain to a user that a particular song was recommended because it shares similar genre attributes or is performed by the same artist as songs the user has previously liked. This transparency fosters user trust and confidence in the system, as users can understand the reasoning behind the recommendations and feel assured that their preferences are being accurately considered.

Despite these advantages, content-based filtering faces several challenges that can impact its effectiveness. One notable challenge is the potential for over-specialization, where the system repeatedly recommends items that are too similar to those the user has already interacted with. This issue arises because content-based filtering relies heavily on the attributes of previously liked items, potentially limiting the diversity of recommendations. For instance, if a user has shown a preference for a specific genre of books, the system might continue to recommend books within that genre, neglecting other genres that the user might also find interesting. Over time, this can lead to a narrow and monotonous set of recommendations, reducing the opportunity for users to discover new and diverse content.

Data sparsity is another significant challenge in content-based filtering. In many practical applications, the attributes of items may not be fully detailed or consistently available, leading to incomplete feature representations. This sparsity can undermine the system's ability to accurately compare items and generate meaningful recommendations. For instance, in a news recommendation system, if the articles lack comprehensive metadata or well-defined keywords, the system may struggle to identify relevant articles that match the user's interests. Addressing this challenge requires robust feature extraction techniques and the integration of supplementary data sources to enrich the feature set.

The effectiveness of content-based filtering is also heavily dependent on the quality and granularity of the features used to represent items. Extensive feature engineering is often required to ensure that the attributes accurately capture the essence of the items and reflect user preferences. This process can be complex and time-consuming, particularly for unstructured data such as text, images, or audio. Advanced techniques such as natural language processing (NLP) and deep learning are often employed to extract meaningful features from unstructured data, enhancing the richness and relevance of the recommendations. For example, NLP techniques can be used to analyze and categorize the themes and sentiments in user reviews or article content, providing deeper insights into user preferences.

In practical applications, hybrid recommender systems are often employed to mitigate the limitations of content-based filtering. By combining content-based filtering with collaborative filtering and other techniques, hybrid systems leverage the strengths of multiple approaches to enhance recommendation accuracy and diversity. For instance, a hybrid system might use collaborative filtering to identify items that are popular among similar users and content-based filtering to ensure that these items align with the user's specific preferences. This integration can address issues related to over-specialization and data sparsity, providing a more balanced and comprehensive recommendation set.

Moreover, the dynamic nature of user preferences necessitates continuous refinement and updating of the recommendation model. As users interact with new items and their preferences evolve, the system must adapt to these changes to maintain the accuracy and relevance of the recommendations. Techniques such as online learning and reinforcement learning can facilitate this dynamic updating process, enabling the system to learn from new interactions in real-time and adjust the recommendations accordingly. For example, an e-commerce platform might use reinforcement learning to optimize the sequence of product recommendations, maximizing the likelihood of purchase by adapting to the user's interactions.

In conclusion, content-based filtering offers significant advantages in terms of personalization, cold start mitigation, and transparency, making it a valuable approach in recommender systems. However, it also faces challenges related to over-specialization, data sparsity, and the need for extensive feature engineering. By understanding and addressing these challenges, developers can enhance the effectiveness of content-based filtering and create robust recommendation systems that deliver relevant and engaging suggestions. The integration of hybrid approaches and advanced machine learning techniques further enriches the capabilities of these systems, ensuring that they remain dynamic and responsive to user needs in an increasingly complex and data-rich environment. Through continuous innovation and refinement, content-based filtering will continue to play a critical role in the development of sophisticated and personalized recommender systems.

5.7. Real-World Applications

Content-based filtering has been widely adopted across various industries, demonstrating its versatility and effectiveness in delivering personalized recommendations. The practical applications of this technique span numerous domains, from e-commerce and entertainment to education and healthcare. Each application leverages the core principles of content-based filtering, tailored to the specific characteristics and requirements of the domain, to enhance user experience, drive engagement, and achieve strategic business objectives.

In the realm of e-commerce, content-based filtering plays a critical role in personalizing the shopping experience. Online retailers such as Amazon utilize this technique to recommend products that align with a user's browsing history, purchase patterns, and explicit preferences. For instance, if a user frequently purchases electronic gadgets, the recommendation system might suggest related items such as accessories, complementary products, or new releases in the same category. This personalized approach not only enhances user satisfaction by presenting relevant products but also increases the likelihood of cross-selling and up-selling, thereby boosting sales and customer loyalty. The recommendation algorithm typically analyzes product features, such as brand, specifications, and user reviews, to identify items that closely match the user's profile, ensuring that the suggestions are pertinent and appealing.

In the entertainment industry, content-based filtering is extensively used by streaming services like Netflix and Spotify to tailor content recommendations to individual users. These platforms analyze the attributes of movies, TV shows, and music tracks—such as genre, cast, director, tempo, and lyrical themes—to construct detailed user profiles and deliver personalized content. For example, Netflix employs sophisticated algorithms that consider a user's viewing history, including the types of genres and actors they favor, to recommend similar movies and shows. This method enhances user retention by continuously providing fresh and relevant content that aligns with the user's tastes. Similarly, Spotify uses content-based filtering to recommend songs and artists that match a user's listening habits, facilitating music discovery and keeping users engaged on the platform.

Education is another domain where content-based filtering has made significant inroads, particularly in personalized learning environments. Educational platforms like Coursera and Khan Academy use this technique to recommend courses, reading materials, and learning resources that align with a student's interests and academic goals. By analyzing the features of educational content—such as subject matter, difficulty level, and format—the system can suggest resources that are most likely to benefit the student. For instance, a student who frequently engages with introductory courses in computer science might be recommended more advanced topics or related fields like data science and artificial intelligence. This personalized approach not only enhances the learning experience but also supports the student in achieving their educational objectives by providing targeted and relevant content.

In the healthcare sector, content-based filtering is employed to personalize patient care and health information delivery. Health platforms and applications analyze patient data, including medical history, treatment preferences, and current health conditions, to recommend personalized health resources, treatment options, and lifestyle changes. For example, a patient with diabetes might receive recommendations for articles on managing blood sugar levels, diet plans tailored to diabetic needs, and exercise routines suitable for their condition. By leveraging detailed patient profiles and the attributes of health resources, content-based filtering can provide tailored advice that enhances patient engagement and supports better health outcomes. This personalized approach is particularly valuable in managing chronic conditions, where ongoing education and support are crucial for effective disease management.

The financial industry also benefits from content-based filtering through personalized financial advice and investment recommendations. Financial platforms analyze user data, such as transaction history, investment preferences, and risk tolerance, to provide tailored recommendations for investment opportunities, savings plans, and budgeting advice. For instance, a user who frequently invests in technology stocks might be recommended new tech companies or mutual funds that align with their investment strategy. By considering the attributes of financial products and aligning them with user profiles, content-based filtering helps users make informed decisions that match their financial goals and risk appetite.

Despite its widespread adoption and success, content-based filtering is not without its challenges in real-world applications. One significant issue is the potential for over-specialization, where the system repeatedly recommends items that are too similar to those the user has already interacted with, limiting exposure to new and diverse content. This challenge can be addressed by integrating content-based filtering with collaborative filtering techniques in hybrid systems, which balance personalization with diversity by leveraging the preferences of similar users. For instance, a hybrid recommendation system might use collaborative filtering to identify popular items among users with similar profiles and content-based filtering to ensure these items align with the user's specific tastes, providing a more comprehensive and varied recommendation set.

Another challenge is the dependency on high-quality and comprehensive feature data. The effectiveness of content-based filtering is heavily reliant on the availability and accuracy of item attributes. In domains where item features are not well-defined or consistently available, the performance of the recommendation system can be compromised. To mitigate this, advanced feature extraction techniques, such as natural language processing (NLP) for text data and computer vision for image data, are employed to enrich the feature set and improve recommendation accuracy. For example, in a news recommendation system, NLP techniques can analyze the content of articles to extract keywords and topics, ensuring that the system can recommend relevant news stories even in the absence of explicit metadata.

The continuous evolution of user preferences also necessitates dynamic updating and refinement of user profiles and recommendation models. As users interact with new items and their interests evolve, the system must adapt to these changes to maintain the relevance and accuracy of the recommendations. Techniques such as online learning and reinforcement learning are increasingly used to enable real-time updating of recommendation models, allowing the system to learn from new interactions and adjust the recommendations accordingly. For instance, an e-commerce platform might use reinforcement learning to optimize the sequence of product recommendations, maximizing the likelihood of purchase by adapting to the user's real-time interactions.

In conclusion, content-based filtering has proven to be a versatile and effective technique across various real-world applications, from e-commerce and entertainment to education and healthcare. By leveraging detailed item attributes and constructing comprehensive user profiles, this approach provides personalized and relevant recommendations that enhance user experience and drive engagement. However, addressing challenges related to over-specialization, data quality, and dynamic user preferences is crucial for maximizing the effectiveness of content-based filtering. The integration of hybrid approaches and advanced machine learning techniques further enriches the capabilities of these systems, ensuring that they remain responsive and adaptive to user needs in an increasingly data-driven world. Through continuous innovation and refinement, content-based filtering will continue to play a pivotal role in the development of sophisticated and personalized recommender systems.

5.8. Conclusion

The exploration of content-based filtering within the broader framework of recommender systems underscores its critical role in enhancing user experience through personalized recommendations. Content-based filtering distinguishes itself by leveraging the intrinsic attributes of items to generate suggestions that closely align with individual user preferences. This method is grounded in the analysis of item features and user interactions, facilitating a highly personalized and transparent recommendation process. The effectiveness of this approach is evident across diverse domains, including e-commerce, entertainment, education, and healthcare, where it significantly contributes to user satisfaction and engagement.

One of the fundamental strengths of content-based filtering lies in its ability to provide tailored recommendations from the onset, thereby addressing the cold start problem that often plagues collaborative filtering systems. By relying on item attributes rather than user interaction data, content-based filtering can recommend new items immediately upon their introduction. For instance, in a movie recommendation system, newly released films can be suggested to users based on their preferred genres, directors, and actors, even if these films have not yet accumulated substantial user ratings. This capability ensures that the system remains dynamic and responsive, continuously offering fresh and relevant content to users.

Furthermore, content-based filtering excels in transparency and explainability, which are crucial for fostering user trust and confidence. The explicit nature of item attributes allows the system to articulate the rationale behind each recommendation clearly. For example, a music recommendation system can explain that a particular song was suggested because it shares genre attributes or thematic elements with songs the user has previously enjoyed. This level of transparency not only enhances user satisfaction but also encourages continued engagement by providing users with insights into the recommendation process.

Despite its advantages, content-based filtering is not without its challenges. Over-specialization remains a significant concern, as the system tends to recommend items that are closely aligned with past user interactions, potentially limiting the diversity of the recommendations. This issue can lead to a monotonous user experience, where the opportunity to explore new and varied content is constrained. To mitigate this, hybrid recommender systems that integrate content-based filtering with collaborative filtering techniques are often employed. These systems leverage the strengths of both approaches, combining the precision of content-based filtering with the serendipity and diversity provided by collaborative filtering. For example, a hybrid system might recommend popular items among similar users while ensuring that these items align with the user's specific preferences, thereby offering a balanced and varied set of suggestions.

Data sparsity and the quality of item features also present significant challenges. The effectiveness of content-based filtering is heavily dependent on the availability and richness of item attributes. In domains where item features are not well-defined or consistently available, the performance of the recommendation system can be compromised. Advanced feature extraction techniques, such as natural language processing (NLP) for text data and computer vision for image data, are essential for addressing this challenge. For instance, NLP can be used to analyze and extract meaningful features from unstructured text, such as user reviews or article content, enriching the feature set and enhancing recommendation accuracy.

The dynamic nature of user preferences necessitates continuous refinement and updating of user profiles and recommendation models. As users interact with new items and their tastes evolve, the system must adapt to these changes to maintain the relevance and accuracy of the recommendations. Techniques such as online learning and reinforcement learning enable real-time updating of recommendation models, allowing the system to learn from new interactions and adjust the recommendations accordingly. For example, an e-commerce platform might use reinforcement learning to optimize the sequence of product recommendations, maximizing the likelihood of purchase by adapting to the user's real-time interactions and preferences.

In practical applications, the integration of contextual information further enhances the relevance and timeliness of recommendations. Contextual factors such as the user's location, time of day, and current activity can significantly influence their preferences and behavior. By incorporating this information, content-based filtering systems can provide more relevant and contextually appropriate recommendations. For instance, a restaurant recommendation app might suggest dining options based on the user's current location and the time of day, offering timely and relevant suggestions that enhance the user experience.

In conclusion, content-based filtering is a powerful and versatile approach to personalized recommendations, offering significant advantages in terms of personalization, transparency, and cold start mitigation. However, addressing challenges related to over-specialization, data sparsity, and dynamic user preferences is crucial for maximizing its effectiveness. The integration of hybrid approaches and advanced machine learning techniques, along with the incorporation of contextual information, further enriches the capabilities of content-based filtering systems. By continuously evolving and adapting to user needs, these systems can deliver personalized and engaging recommendations that drive user satisfaction and loyalty across various domains. Through a deep understanding of its principles, challenges, and applications, developers can harness the full potential of content-based filtering to create sophisticated and effective recommender systems in an increasingly data-driven world.

6. Hybrid Recommender Systems

Hybrid recommender systems represent the next evolution in recommendation technology, combining multiple approaches to leverage their individual strengths while mitigating their weaknesses. By integrating collaborative filtering, content-based filtering, and other techniques, hybrid systems can provide more accurate, diverse, and robust recommendations. This chapter delves into the various hybridization strategies, their implementation, and practical applications, supported by real-world case studies.

6.1. Motivation for Hybrid Methods

The evolution of recommender systems has been driven by the quest for greater accuracy, relevance, and user satisfaction. Despite the considerable advancements achieved through content-based and collaborative filtering techniques, each approach inherently possesses limitations that can hinder its effectiveness. This realization has catalyzed the development and adoption of hybrid methods, which seek to amalgamate the strengths of multiple recommendation strategies while mitigating their individual weaknesses. The motivation for hybrid methods arises from the need to enhance the robustness, diversity, and scalability of recommender systems, ensuring that they deliver personalized and engaging experiences across diverse applications.

One of the primary motivations for hybrid methods is the desire to address the cold start problem, a significant challenge for both content-based and collaborative filtering systems. The cold start problem manifests when new users or items are introduced to the system, lacking sufficient interaction data to generate accurate recommendations. Content-based filtering, while effective in leveraging item attributes to recommend new items, can struggle when user profiles are sparse or when item features are incomplete. Conversely, collaborative filtering relies heavily on user interactions and can fail to provide meaningful recommendations for new users or items with limited ratings. By combining content-based and collaborative filtering approaches, hybrid methods can leverage the strengths of both techniques, utilizing item attributes to inform initial recommendations and user interactions to refine them over time. For example, a hybrid system might use content-based filtering to recommend new movies to a user based on their stated genre preferences and then refine these recommendations using collaborative filtering as the user begins to rate and review films.

Another key motivation for hybrid methods is the need to overcome the limitations of over-specialization and sparsity. Over-specialization occurs when a recommendation system repeatedly suggests items that are too similar to those the user has already encountered, limiting the diversity of the recommendations and potentially leading to user fatigue. Content-based filtering, which focuses on the attributes of previously liked items, is particularly susceptible to this issue. Collaborative filtering, while providing a broader range of suggestions based on the preferences of similar users, can suffer from data sparsity, especially in systems with a vast catalog of items and relatively few interactions. Hybrid methods can address these limitations by integrating the precision of content-based recommendations with the diversity and user-centric insights provided by collaborative filtering. For instance, a music recommendation system might initially use content-based filtering to suggest songs with similar attributes to those the user enjoys and then diversify the recommendations by incorporating tracks popular among users with similar listening habits.

The pursuit of enhanced recommendation accuracy and relevance further motivates the adoption of hybrid methods. Both content-based and collaborative filtering systems are vulnerable to biases and inaccuracies inherent in their respective data sources. Content-based filtering can be limited by the quality and completeness of item attributes, while collaborative filtering can be skewed by the popularity bias, where widely-rated items dominate the recommendations at the expense of niche content. By combining these approaches, hybrid methods can provide a more balanced and nuanced understanding of user preferences, improving the overall accuracy of the recommendations. For example, an e-commerce platform might use content-based filtering to recommend products based on detailed descriptions and user reviews, while also incorporating collaborative filtering to highlight items that have been well-received by similar customers. This dual approach ensures that the recommendations are both relevant to the user's stated interests and reflective of broader user trends.

Scalability and computational efficiency are additional factors driving the motivation for hybrid methods. As the number of users and items in a system grows, the computational demands of generating real-time recommendations can become prohibitive. Content-based filtering, which relies on precomputed item attributes, can offer efficiency in feature extraction and similarity computation, while collaborative filtering can leverage user interaction data to dynamically adjust recommendations. Hybrid methods can optimize the balance between these computational demands, ensuring that the system remains responsive and scalable. For instance, a hybrid recommendation system might precompute item similarities using content-based filtering and then use collaborative filtering to dynamically adjust the recommendations based on real-time user interactions. This approach leverages the computational efficiency of content-based methods while maintaining the flexibility and adaptability of collaborative filtering.

The integration of advanced machine learning techniques further enhances the potential of hybrid methods. Deep learning models, such as neural collaborative filtering and autoencoders, can capture complex, non-linear relationships between users and items, providing more accurate and personalized recommendations. These

74

models can be combined with traditional content-based and collaborative filtering approaches to form sophisticated hybrid systems that leverage the strengths of each technique. For example, a hybrid recommendation system might use a deep learning model to extract high-level features from item descriptions and user interactions, which are then used to inform both content-based and collaborative filtering components. This integration enhances the system's ability to understand and predict user preferences, resulting in more nuanced and effective recommendations.

In practical applications, hybrid methods have demonstrated significant improvements in user satisfaction and engagement. For instance, Netflix employs a hybrid recommendation system that combines content-based filtering, collaborative filtering, and machine learning models to deliver personalized movie and TV show suggestions. This multi-faceted approach allows Netflix to provide recommendations that are not only tailored to individual user preferences but also reflective of broader viewing trends, enhancing the overall user experience. Similarly, e-commerce platforms like Amazon use hybrid methods to recommend products by integrating user browsing history, purchase patterns, and product attributes, ensuring that the suggestions are both relevant and diverse.

In conclusion, the motivation for hybrid methods in recommender systems is driven by the need to enhance accuracy, relevance, and diversity while addressing the inherent limitations of individual recommendation techniques. By combining content-based and collaborative filtering approaches, hybrid methods leverage the strengths of each technique to provide a more robust and comprehensive understanding of user preferences. The integration of advanced machine learning models further enriches the capabilities of hybrid systems, enabling them to capture complex patterns and deliver highly personalized recommendations. Through continuous innovation and refinement, hybrid methods will continue to play a pivotal role in the development of sophisticated recommender systems that meet the evolving needs and preferences of users in an increasingly data-driven world.

6.2. Types of Hybrid Recommender Systems

Hybrid recommender systems represent a sophisticated synthesis of multiple recommendation techniques, designed to leverage the strengths and mitigate the weaknesses of individual methods. By combining different approaches, hybrid systems can provide more accurate, diverse, and robust recommendations, thereby enhancing user satisfaction and engagement. The types of hybrid recommender systems vary based on how the different techniques are integrated, each with its own unique advantages and complexities. Understanding these types and their underlying mechanisms is crucial for developing effective and versatile recommendation systems.

One common type of hybrid recommender system is the **weighted hybrid**, where the scores from multiple recommendation techniques are combined using a weighted sum to produce the final recommendation. In this approach, each recommendation method (such as content-based filtering, collaborative filtering, and others) generates a score indicating the relevance of an item to a user. These scores are then aggregated, with each method's contribution weighted according to its perceived reliability or relevance. For instance, in a movie recommendation system, the weighted hybrid approach might combine the content-based score derived from movie attributes (e.g., genre, director) with the collaborative filtering score based on user ratings. The final score for a movie could be expressed as:

$$\text{Final Score}(u, i)$$
$$= w_1 \times \text{Content-Based Score}(u, i) + w_2$$
$$\times \text{Collaborative Filtering Score}(u, i)$$

where w_1 and w_2 are the weights assigned to the content-based and collaborative filtering scores, respectively. This method allows for flexible adjustment of the weights to optimize the balance between different recommendation sources, enhancing the system's overall performance.

Another prevalent type is the **switching hybrid**, which dynamically selects the most appropriate recommendation method based on specific criteria or contextual factors. In this approach, the system switches between different recommendation techniques depending on the user's profile, the item's characteristics, or the context of the recommendation. For example, a music streaming service might use content-based filtering for new users with sparse interaction data, relying on song attributes like genre and artist to generate recommendations. As the user interacts more with the platform, the system might switch to collaborative filtering, leveraging the user's growing listening history to provide more personalized suggestions. This dynamic switching ensures that the most suitable recommendation method is applied at each stage, improving the system's adaptability and effectiveness.

The **mixed hybrid** approach, also known as the mixed ensemble, simultaneously presents recommendations generated by multiple methods, allowing users to choose from a diverse set of suggestions. This type of hybrid system aggregates the outputs from different recommendation techniques and displays them side by side, providing users with a variety of options. For instance, an e-commerce platform might present product recommendations from a content-based system alongside those from a collaborative filtering system. Users can then select from items that match their browsing history, product reviews, and preferences of similar users. This approach not only enhances the diversity of the recommendations but also empowers users to explore different aspects of their preferences.

Feature augmentation hybrid systems enhance the capabilities of one recommendation method by incorporating features derived from another. In this type, the output of one recommendation technique is used to augment the input features of another, creating a more enriched dataset for generating recommendations. For example, a movie recommendation system might use collaborative filtering to identify user preferences and then incorporate these preferences as additional features in a content-based filtering model. This combination can improve the granularity and accuracy of the recommendations by leveraging the strengths of both methods. Mathematically, if $\mathbf{f}_{cb}(i)$ represents the content-based features of item i and $\mathbf{f}_{cf}(u)$ represents the collaborative filtering features of user u, the augmented feature vector $\mathbf{f}_{aug}(u, i)$ might be expressed as:

$$\mathbf{f}_{aug}(u, i) = [\mathbf{f}_{cb}(i), \mathbf{f}_{cf}(u)]$$

This enriched feature vector provides a more comprehensive basis for generating recommendations, enhancing the system's overall performance.

Cascade hybrid systems operate by sequentially applying multiple recommendation techniques, where the output of one method is refined by subsequent methods. In this approach, an initial set of recommendations is generated using one technique and then re-ranked or filtered by another. For instance, a news recommendation system might first use content-based filtering to generate an initial list of relevant articles based on a user's reading history. This list is then refined using collaborative filtering, which re-ranks the articles based on the preferences of similar users. This cascading process ensures that the final recommendations are both relevant and personalized, combining the strengths of different methods.

Another sophisticated type is the **meta-level hybrid**, where the model generated by one recommendation method is used as the input for another. In this approach, the internal representation of user preferences or item attributes created by one technique serves as the foundation for another technique. For example, a deep learning model might be used to learn latent features from user interactions, and these features are then fed into a collaborative filtering model to generate recommendations. This method leverages the complex feature extraction capabilities of advanced models to enhance the accuracy and depth of the recommendations.

Hybrid systems using deep learning and advanced machine learning techniques represent the frontier of recommender system development. These systems integrate neural networks, such as convolutional neural networks (CNNs) and recurrent neural networks (RNNs), with traditional recommendation methods to capture complex, non-linear relationships between users and items. For instance, neural collaborative filtering combines the principles of collaborative filtering with the representation learning capabilities of neural networks, enabling the system to model intricate user-item interactions. The neural network learns to predict user preferences by optimizing a loss function that minimizes the error between predicted and actual ratings, thereby enhancing the accuracy of the recommendations.

In practical applications, the choice of hybrid method depends on the specific needs and constraints of the domain. For example, Netflix employs a sophisticated hybrid system that combines collaborative filtering, content-based filtering, and machine learning models to deliver personalized movie and TV show recommendations. This multi-faceted approach allows Netflix to provide recommendations that are both tailored to individual user preferences and reflective of broader viewing trends, enhancing the overall user experience. Similarly, e-commerce platforms like Amazon use hybrid methods to recommend products by integrating user browsing history, purchase patterns, and product attributes, ensuring that the suggestions are both relevant and diverse.

The implications of using hybrid recommender systems are profound, as they offer a balanced approach that leverages the strengths of multiple techniques while mitigating their individual weaknesses. Hybrid methods enhance the robustness and accuracy of recommendations, ensuring that the system can adapt to different user needs and contexts. By combining the precision of content-based filtering with the diversity and user-centric insights provided by collaborative filtering, hybrid systems deliver a more comprehensive and satisfying user experience. Additionally, the integration of advanced machine learning models further enriches the capabilities of these systems, enabling them to capture complex patterns and deliver highly personalized recommendations.

In conclusion, the various types of hybrid recommender systems represent a sophisticated evolution in the field of recommendation technologies. By combining different techniques in diverse ways, these systems enhance the accuracy, diversity, and robustness of recommendations, ultimately leading to improved user satisfaction and engagement. The continuous development and refinement of hybrid methods, driven by advancements in machine learning and data analytics, promise to further elevate the effectiveness of recommender systems in an increasingly data-driven world. Through a deep understanding of the types and mechanisms of hybrid recommender systems, developers can create powerful and versatile solutions that meet the evolving needs of users across various domains.

6.3. Case Studies and Practical Applications

The application of hybrid recommender systems in real-world scenarios exemplifies their profound impact on user engagement and satisfaction across diverse industries. By integrating multiple recommendation techniques, these systems overcome the limitations inherent in singular approaches, providing more accurate, diverse, and personalized recommendations. This section delves into several case studies and practical applications, illustrating how hybrid recommender systems are employed to address specific challenges and enhance user experiences.

One of the most prominent examples of hybrid recommender systems in practice is Netflix, a leader in streaming entertainment. Netflix utilizes a sophisticated hybrid approach that combines collaborative filtering, content-based filtering, and advanced machine learning models to deliver highly personalized movie and TV show recommendations. The collaborative filtering component analyzes the viewing patterns of millions of users to identify those with similar tastes, thereby suggesting content that has been well-received by similar viewers. Concurrently, the content-based filtering component evaluates the attributes of movies and shows, such as genre, cast, and director, to recommend content that aligns with a user's explicit preferences. This dual approach is further enhanced by machine learning algorithms that continuously refine the recommendation model based on user interactions. For instance, neural collaborative filtering and recurrent neural networks (RNNs) capture complex temporal patterns in user behavior, optimizing recommendations over time. The result is a seamless and engaging user experience, where recommendations evolve dynamically with user preferences, keeping the content fresh and relevant.

In the e-commerce domain, Amazon exemplifies the effective application of hybrid recommender systems to enhance the shopping experience. Amazon's recommendation engine integrates user browsing history, purchase patterns, and product attributes to generate personalized product suggestions. The collaborative filtering component leverages the collective purchasing behavior of users to identify products frequently bought together, while the content-based filtering component uses product descriptions, reviews, and metadata to recommend items that match a user's specific interests. For example, if a user frequently buys electronic gadgets, the system might suggest complementary products such as accessories and related devices. Additionally, Amazon employs advanced techniques like matrix factorization to uncover latent factors in user-item interactions, improving the accuracy of recommendations. This hybrid approach not only increases the likelihood of cross-selling and up-selling but also enhances customer satisfaction by providing relevant and diverse product options.

Another compelling case study is Spotify, which employs hybrid recommender systems to curate personalized music experiences for its users. Spotify combines collaborative filtering, content-based filtering, and deep learning models to recommend songs and artists. The collaborative filtering component analyzes user listening patterns and preferences, identifying users with similar musical tastes to suggest new tracks. Simultaneously, the content-based filtering component evaluates the attributes of songs, such as genre, tempo, and lyrical themes, to recommend music that aligns with the user's existing preferences. Deep learning models, such as convolutional neural networks (CNNs), are used to analyze audio features and capture the nuanced aspects of musical content. For instance, a CNN might be trained to recognize the acoustic patterns of different genres, enabling the system to recommend songs with similar sound profiles. This multi-faceted approach ensures that users receive a rich and varied music discovery experience, tailored to their evolving tastes and preferences.

In the realm of online education, platforms like Coursera and Khan Academy leverage hybrid recommender systems to personalize learning experiences. These platforms integrate content-based filtering and collaborative filtering to recommend courses, reading materials, and educational resources. The content-based filtering component analyzes the attributes of educational content, such as subject matter, difficulty level, and instructional format, to match resources with a student's learning profile. Collaborative filtering identifies patterns in the learning behaviors of similar students, suggesting courses and materials that have been effective for peers with comparable academic goals. For instance, a student who has completed several introductory computer science courses might be recommended advanced topics in data science and machine learning. This hybrid approach enhances the educational experience by providing personalized learning paths that cater to individual needs and aspirations, fostering better learning outcomes and student satisfaction.

Healthcare applications also benefit significantly from hybrid recommender systems. Health platforms and applications use these systems to provide personalized health recommendations, treatment options, and lifestyle advice. The content-based filtering component analyzes patient data, such as medical history, treatment preferences, and current health conditions, to recommend tailored health resources and interventions. Collaborative filtering leverages the experiences of similar patients to suggest treatments and lifestyle changes that have proven effective for others with similar health profiles. For example, a patient managing diabetes might receive personalized recommendations for diet plans, exercise routines, and medication based on the successful management strategies of other diabetic patients. This personalized approach supports better health outcomes by providing patients with relevant and actionable health advice, tailored to their unique needs and circumstances.

The implications of these case studies are profound, highlighting the transformative potential of hybrid recommender systems across various domains. By integrating multiple recommendation techniques, these systems enhance the accuracy, diversity, and personalization of recommendations, driving user engagement and satisfaction. The continuous refinement and adaptation of hybrid models, fueled by advancements in machine learning and data analytics, ensure that recommender systems remain responsive to evolving user preferences and contexts. Moreover, the practical applications of hybrid recommender systems demonstrate their versatility and effectiveness in addressing specific challenges and achieving strategic business objectives.

In conclusion, the case studies and practical applications of hybrid recommender systems underscore their critical role in enhancing user experiences across diverse industries. By combining the strengths of content-based filtering, collaborative filtering, and advanced machine learning models, hybrid systems deliver highly personalized and relevant recommendations that drive engagement and satisfaction. The continuous evolution and refinement of these systems, guided by real-world applications and user feedback, promise to further elevate the effectiveness of recommender systems in an increasingly data-driven world. Through a deep understanding of the mechanisms and benefits of hybrid recommender systems, developers can create sophisticated and versatile solutions that meet the dynamic needs and preferences of users across various domains.

6.4. Implementation Strategies

Implementing hybrid recommender systems involves a sophisticated blend of multiple recommendation techniques, each contributing unique strengths to address specific limitations. This implementation requires careful planning, selection of appropriate algorithms, integration of various data sources, and continuous refinement to ensure optimal performance. Effective implementation strategies are pivotal in leveraging the full potential of hybrid systems, thereby enhancing user satisfaction and engagement across diverse applications.

The first step in implementing a hybrid recommender system is the selection of suitable algorithms that complement each other. This involves choosing a combination of content-based filtering, collaborative filtering, and possibly other advanced techniques such as matrix factorization or deep learning models. The choice of algorithms depends on the nature of the data, the specific requirements of the application, and the desired outcomes. For instance, in an e-commerce platform, content-based filtering might be employed to analyze product attributes and user reviews, while collaborative filtering leverages user interaction data to identify patterns in purchasing behavior. The integration of these algorithms can be achieved through various hybridization techniques, such as weighted hybrids, switching hybrids, and meta-level hybrids, each offering distinct advantages in different contexts.

Weighted hybrid systems combine the scores from multiple recommendation techniques using a weighted sum to produce the final recommendation. This approach requires determining the optimal weights for each technique, which can be achieved through empirical testing and optimization. For example, in a movie recommendation system, the final recommendation score for a movie i for user u might be calculated as:

$$\text{Score}(u, i) = w_1 \times \text{Content-Based Score}(u, i) + w_2 \\ \times \text{Collaborative Filtering Score}(u, i) + w_3 \\ \times \text{Matrix Factorization Score}(u, i)$$

where w_1, w_2, and w_3 are the weights assigned to the content-based, collaborative filtering, and matrix factorization scores, respectively. These weights can be optimized using techniques such as cross-validation, where the performance of different weight combinations is evaluated on a validation dataset to identify the configuration that maximizes recommendation accuracy.

Switching hybrid systems dynamically select the most appropriate recommendation technique based on specific criteria or contextual factors. This approach involves developing a decision-making framework that determines when to switch between techniques. For instance, a music streaming service might use content-based filtering for new users with sparse interaction data and switch to collaborative filtering as the user's listening history grows. The decision criteria can be based on

81

factors such as the amount of user interaction data, the type of item being recommended, or the user's current context (e.g., location, time of day). Implementing switching hybrids requires robust logic and infrastructure to support real-time decision-making and seamless transitions between recommendation techniques.

Meta-level hybrid systems use the model generated by one recommendation technique as the input for another. This approach often involves training complex models that can capture high-level patterns and relationships in the data. For example, a deep learning model might be used to extract latent features from user-item interactions, which are then fed into a collaborative filtering algorithm to generate recommendations. Implementing meta-level hybrids requires advanced machine learning expertise and computational resources, as these models can be computationally intensive and require large datasets for training. However, the resulting models can provide highly accurate and nuanced recommendations, leveraging the strengths of multiple techniques in a unified framework.

Feature augmentation hybrids enhance the capabilities of one recommendation method by incorporating features derived from another. This approach involves enriching the feature set used by a recommendation technique with additional information extracted from other methods. For instance, a movie recommendation system might augment the content-based features of movies with collaborative filtering features that capture user preferences. The augmented feature vector $\mathbf{f}_{aug}(u, i)$ for user u and movie i might be expressed as:

$$\mathbf{f}_{aug}(u, i) = [\mathbf{f}_{cb}(i), \mathbf{f}_{cf}(u)]$$

where $\mathbf{f}_{cb}(i)$ represents the content-based features of movie i and $\mathbf{f}_{cf}(u)$ represents the collaborative filtering features of user u. This enriched feature set provides a more comprehensive basis for generating recommendations, improving the accuracy and relevance of the suggestions.

Implementing hybrid recommender systems also involves addressing challenges related to data integration and scalability. Hybrid systems often require combining data from multiple sources, such as user interaction logs, item metadata, and contextual information. This integration can be complex, necessitating robust data processing pipelines that ensure data consistency and quality. Additionally, hybrid systems must be scalable to handle large volumes of data and generate real-time recommendations. This requires efficient algorithms and infrastructure capable of processing and analyzing data at scale. Techniques such as parallel processing, distributed computing, and cloud-based architectures can be employed to achieve the necessary scalability.

Continuous refinement and evaluation are critical components of implementing hybrid recommender systems. As user preferences evolve and new data becomes available, the recommendation models must be updated and fine-tuned to maintain their accuracy and relevance. This involves regularly retraining the models, adjusting the hybridization strategies, and conducting rigorous evaluations to assess performance. Evaluation metrics such as precision, recall, F1-score, and mean squared error can be used to quantify the effectiveness of the recommendations and guide further improvements. A/B testing and user feedback can also provide valuable insights into the real-world impact of the recommendations, informing iterative enhancements to the system.

The implications of effectively implementing hybrid recommender systems are far-reaching, significantly enhancing user experience and engagement across various applications. For instance, Netflix's sophisticated hybrid system, which integrates collaborative filtering, content-based filtering, and advanced machine learning models, has been instrumental in retaining users and driving viewer engagement. By continuously refining its recommendation algorithms and incorporating user feedback, Netflix ensures that its recommendations remain relevant and personalized, fostering a loyal user base.

In the e-commerce domain, Amazon's hybrid recommender system leverages multiple techniques to provide personalized product suggestions, enhancing the shopping experience and driving sales. By integrating user browsing history, purchase patterns, and product attributes, Amazon can deliver highly relevant recommendations that encourage cross-selling and up-selling, boosting overall revenue. The continuous refinement and optimization of its hybrid system ensure that Amazon remains at the forefront of personalized e-commerce, setting a benchmark for other platforms.

In conclusion, the implementation of hybrid recommender systems involves a strategic blend of multiple recommendation techniques, data integration, and continuous refinement. By carefully selecting and integrating appropriate algorithms, addressing scalability challenges, and regularly evaluating performance, developers can create robust and effective hybrid systems that enhance user satisfaction and engagement. The practical applications and case studies of hybrid recommender systems in companies like Netflix and Amazon illustrate the profound impact of these systems on user experience and business outcomes. Through a deep understanding of implementation strategies and continuous innovation, hybrid recommender systems will continue to evolve, meeting the dynamic needs and preferences of users in an increasingly data-driven world.

6.5. Conclusion

The exploration of hybrid recommender systems marks a significant milestone in the evolution of personalized recommendation technologies, underscoring their potential to integrate the strengths of various methodologies while addressing their individual limitations. The rationale for hybrid systems lies in their ability to mitigate issues such as the cold start problem, over-specialization, and data sparsity, which often challenge standalone content-based and collaborative filtering techniques. By leveraging the complementary benefits of these methods, hybrid systems provide a more robust, accurate, and diverse recommendation framework that enhances user satisfaction across multiple domains.

One of the critical motivations for adopting hybrid recommender systems is their capacity to deliver superior personalization by combining the precision of content-based filtering with the broad appeal of collaborative filtering. Content-based filtering excels at providing recommendations based on the attributes of items previously liked by the user, ensuring that the suggestions align closely with their explicit preferences. However, this method can suffer from over-specialization, limiting the diversity of recommendations. On the other hand, collaborative filtering leverages the collective preferences of similar users to suggest items, offering a broader perspective and exposing users to new and diverse content. Hybrid systems seamlessly integrate these approaches, using content-based filtering to maintain relevance and collaborative filtering to introduce variety, thereby providing a balanced recommendation experience.

The implementation of hybrid systems is a complex yet rewarding endeavor, requiring meticulous planning, selection of algorithms, and integration of diverse data sources. The choice of hybridization technique—whether weighted, switching, meta-level, or feature augmentation—depends on the specific needs of the application and the nature of the data. For instance, a weighted hybrid might combine the scores from different recommendation methods using a formula like:

$$\text{Score}(u, i) = w_1 \times \text{Content-Based Score}(u, i) + w_2 \\ \times \text{Collaborative Filtering Score}(u, i)$$

where w_1 and w_2 are the weights assigned to the respective methods, optimized through empirical testing to maximize accuracy. Similarly, switching hybrids dynamically select the most suitable recommendation method based on contextual factors, ensuring that the system adapts to different user scenarios and data availability. Meta-level hybrids utilize the model output from one technique as the input for another, enabling advanced feature extraction and pattern recognition, while feature augmentation hybrids enrich the feature set of one method with insights from another, enhancing the recommendation precision.

The successful deployment of hybrid recommender systems is exemplified by industry leaders like Netflix and Amazon, whose sophisticated recommendation engines have set benchmarks in user engagement and satisfaction. Netflix's hybrid system, which integrates collaborative filtering, content-based filtering, and advanced machine learning models, continuously evolves with user interactions, delivering highly personalized and dynamic content suggestions. Similarly, Amazon's recommendation engine leverages user browsing history, purchase patterns, and product attributes to provide relevant and diverse product suggestions, driving significant increases in sales and customer loyalty. These case studies illustrate the profound impact of hybrid systems on enhancing the user experience and achieving strategic business objectives.

Furthermore, the continuous refinement and evaluation of hybrid recommender systems are paramount to maintaining their effectiveness. As user preferences evolve and new data becomes available, the models must be regularly updated and fine-tuned to reflect these changes. Techniques such as online learning and reinforcement learning enable real-time adaptation, ensuring that the recommendations remain current and personalized. For instance, reinforcement learning can optimize the sequence of recommendations by learning from user interactions, thereby maximizing engagement and satisfaction. Evaluation metrics such as precision, recall, and mean squared error provide quantitative measures of performance, guiding further improvements and ensuring that the system meets the desired accuracy and relevance standards.

In conclusion, hybrid recommender systems represent a sophisticated and powerful approach to personalized recommendations, combining the strengths of content-based and collaborative filtering to deliver accurate, diverse, and dynamic suggestions. The successful implementation of these systems involves careful algorithm selection, data integration, and continuous refinement, supported by robust evaluation frameworks. The practical applications of hybrid systems in companies like Netflix and Amazon highlight their transformative potential in enhancing user experience and driving business success. As the field of recommendation technologies continues to evolve, hybrid systems will remain at the forefront, leveraging advancements in machine learning and data analytics to meet the ever-changing needs and preferences of users in an increasingly data-driven world. Through a deep understanding of their principles, implementation strategies, and real-world applications, developers can harness the full potential of hybrid recommender systems to create sophisticated, personalized, and effective recommendation solutions.

7. Advanced Algorithms and Techniques

As recommender systems evolve, advanced algorithms and techniques have emerged to address the increasing complexity and demands of personalization in digital commerce. This chapter delves into the frontier of recommendation technology, exploring deep learning, sequence-based models, attention mechanisms, and reinforcement learning. These cutting-edge approaches offer new possibilities for creating highly personalized and dynamic recommender systems, pushing the boundaries of what traditional methods can achieve.

7.1. Deep Learning for Recommender Systems

Deep learning has emerged as a transformative force in the field of recommender systems, offering sophisticated methods for capturing complex patterns in user behavior and item attributes that traditional approaches may overlook. The advent of deep learning techniques has revolutionized the development and implementation of recommender systems by enabling the modeling of intricate non-linear relationships and providing highly personalized and accurate recommendations. The application of deep learning in recommender systems encompasses various architectures, including neural collaborative filtering, convolutional neural networks (CNNs), recurrent neural networks (RNNs), and autoencoders, each contributing unique advantages to the recommendation process.

At the core of deep learning for recommender systems is the ability to learn rich, high-dimensional representations of users and items from vast amounts of data. This capability is particularly advantageous in dealing with the sparsity and high dimensionality that characterize user-item interaction matrices in collaborative filtering. Traditional matrix factorization techniques, such as Singular Value Decomposition (SVD), approximate the interaction matrix by decomposing it into latent factors. However, deep learning models extend this concept by learning these latent factors through multiple layers of non-linear transformations, allowing for the capture of more complex interactions. Neural collaborative filtering (NCF), for example, replaces the linear inner product used in matrix factorization with a neural network to model user-item interactions, thereby enhancing the flexibility and expressiveness of the model.

$$\hat{r}_{ui} = f(\mathbf{p}_u, \mathbf{q}_i)$$

In NCF, the function f is a neural network that takes the latent factors $\mathbf{p}_u$ (user) and $\mathbf{q}_i$ (item) as inputs, learning a non-linear interaction between them. The network is trained to minimize the error between the predicted rating $\hat{r}_{ui}$ and the actual rating r_{ui}, typically using gradient descent optimization techniques.

Convolutional neural networks (CNNs) have demonstrated significant efficacy in capturing local patterns and hierarchical structures, making them particularly suitable for content-based filtering tasks. In recommender systems, CNNs are often employed to process unstructured data such as images, text, and audio, extracting high-level features that can be used to enhance recommendations. For instance, in a fashion recommendation system, CNNs can analyze product images to identify visual attributes such as color, style, and texture, which are then incorporated into the recommendation model. Similarly, text-based recommendations can benefit from CNNs by extracting semantic features from product descriptions, user reviews, or article content, improving the system's ability to match items with user preferences.

Recurrent neural networks (RNNs) and their advanced variants, such as Long Short-Term Memory (LSTM) networks, are particularly adept at modeling sequential data, capturing temporal dependencies in user interactions. This makes RNNs ideal for applications where the order and timing of interactions are crucial, such as music or video streaming services. For example, an RNN can be used to model the sequence of songs a user listens to, learning the temporal patterns in their listening behavior to predict future preferences. The network's ability to maintain a memory of previous interactions allows it to provide contextually relevant recommendations, enhancing the personalization of the user experience.

Autoencoders, another powerful deep learning architecture, are employed for dimensionality reduction and feature learning. In recommender systems, autoencoders can compress high-dimensional user-item interaction data into a lower-dimensional latent space, capturing essential patterns while reducing noise. This compressed representation can then be used for various recommendation tasks, including collaborative filtering and anomaly detection. Variational autoencoders (VAEs), a probabilistic extension of autoencoders, further enhance this capability by learning a distribution over the latent space, enabling the generation of new, plausible user-item interactions and improving the robustness of the recommendations.

The integration of deep learning techniques into recommender systems has significant implications for the accuracy and personalization of recommendations. By leveraging the powerful feature extraction and representation learning capabilities of deep neural networks, these systems can uncover subtle patterns and relationships that traditional methods may miss. For example, Netflix's recommendation system employs deep learning models to analyze vast amounts of viewing data, capturing complex interactions between users and content to provide highly personalized movie and TV show suggestions. This level of personalization not only enhances user satisfaction but also drives engagement and retention, contributing to the platform's success.

Despite the considerable advantages, implementing deep learning for recommender systems also presents challenges. The complexity and computational demands of training deep neural networks require substantial computational resources and expertise in machine learning. Moreover, the large amounts of data needed to train these models necessitate robust data collection and processing pipelines. Ensuring the interpretability of deep learning models is another challenge, as the intricate non-linear transformations can make it difficult to understand the rationale behind specific recommendations. Addressing these challenges requires a careful balance between model complexity, computational efficiency, and interpretability, often necessitating the use of hybrid approaches that combine deep learning with more traditional techniques.

The continuous evolution of deep learning architectures and techniques promises further advancements in recommender systems. Emerging models such as transformers, which have revolutionized natural language processing, are being adapted for recommendation tasks, offering new ways to capture long-range dependencies and contextual information. Additionally, the integration of reinforcement learning with deep learning opens new avenues for optimizing recommendations over time, learning from user feedback to continuously improve the quality and relevance of suggestions.

In conclusion, deep learning has profoundly transformed recommender systems, providing powerful tools for capturing complex user-item interactions and delivering highly personalized recommendations. By integrating various deep learning architectures, such as neural collaborative filtering, convolutional neural networks, recurrent neural networks, and autoencoders, modern recommender systems can leverage the strengths of these techniques to enhance accuracy, diversity, and user satisfaction. The successful implementation of deep learning in recommender systems, as exemplified by platforms like Netflix, highlights its potential to drive engagement and retention through personalized recommendations. However, the challenges associated with computational complexity, data requirements, and interpretability necessitate ongoing research and innovation to fully realize the potential of deep learning in this field. Through continuous exploration and refinement, deep learning will remain at the forefront of advancements in recommender systems, shaping the future of personalized user experiences in an increasingly data-driven world.

7.2. Attention Mechanisms

Attention mechanisms have revolutionized the landscape of deep learning and, by extension, recommender systems, by enabling models to dynamically focus on the most relevant parts of the input data. Originally introduced in the context of neural machine translation, attention mechanisms have since been adapted to a wide range of tasks, including image processing, speech recognition, and, notably, recommendation systems. By allowing models to weigh the importance of different elements in the input, attention mechanisms facilitate the capture of intricate relationships and dependencies that traditional models might overlook, thereby enhancing the accuracy and personalization of recommendations.

At its core, an attention mechanism computes a weighted sum of input features, where the weights, or attention scores, indicate the relevance of each feature to the task at hand. This process can be mathematically represented as follows. Given an input sequence $\mathbf{X} = [\mathbf{x}_1, \mathbf{x}_2, ..., \mathbf{x}_n]$ and a query vector $\mathbf{q}$, the attention mechanism calculates a set of attention weights α_i for each input element $\mathbf{x}_i$. These weights are typically derived using a compatibility function $\text{score}(\mathbf{q}, \mathbf{x}_i)$, which measures the similarity between the query and the input element. A common choice for the compatibility function is the dot product:

$$\alpha_i = \frac{\exp(\mathbf{q}^\top \mathbf{x}_i)}{\sum_{j=1}^{n} \exp(\mathbf{q}^\top \mathbf{x}_j)}$$

The attention weights are then used to compute the context vector $\mathbf{c}$, which is a weighted sum of the input elements:

$$\mathbf{c} = \sum_{i=1}^{n} \alpha_i \mathbf{x}_i$$

This context vector $\mathbf{c}$ encapsulates the most relevant information from the input sequence, allowing the model to focus on the critical aspects when generating the output.

In recommender systems, attention mechanisms can be employed to enhance both user modeling and item representation. For instance, in user modeling, an attention-based approach can dynamically weigh the importance of a user's past interactions when predicting future preferences. This is particularly useful in capturing the temporal dynamics and varying significance of different interactions. For example, in a music recommendation system, recent listening history might be more indicative of current preferences than older interactions. By applying an attention mechanism, the model can assign higher weights to recent interactions, ensuring that the recommendations reflect the user's evolving tastes.

Similarly, attention mechanisms can be used to improve item representation by focusing on the most salient features. In a movie recommendation system, for instance, different aspects such as genre, director, and cast might vary in importance depending on the user's preferences. An attention-based model can learn to emphasize the features that are most relevant to each user, thereby providing more personalized recommendations. This dynamic weighting of features enhances the model's flexibility and adaptability, allowing it to cater to diverse user preferences more effectively.

Transformer models, which are built upon attention mechanisms, have set new benchmarks in various domains, including recommender systems. The self-attention mechanism, a cornerstone of transformers, computes attention weights for each element in the input sequence relative to all other elements, enabling the capture of long-range dependencies and complex interactions. The self-attention mechanism is defined as follows. Given an input sequence **X**, the model computes three matrices: queries **Q**, keys **K**, and values **V**. The attention weights are calculated using the scaled dot-product attention:

$$Attention(\mathbf{Q}, \mathbf{K}, \mathbf{V}) = softmax\left(\frac{\mathbf{Q}\mathbf{K}^\top}{\sqrt{d_k}}\right)\mathbf{V}$$

where d_k is the dimensionality of the keys. This mechanism allows the model to weigh the importance of each input element based on its relevance to others, capturing intricate relationships that are crucial for generating accurate recommendations.

In practical applications, attention mechanisms have demonstrated substantial improvements in recommendation performance. For example, in session-based recommendation systems, where the goal is to predict the next item a user will interact with based on their current session, attention mechanisms can effectively capture the sequential dependencies and contextual relevance of past interactions. By focusing on the most relevant items within the session, the model can provide more accurate and contextually appropriate recommendations.

Another notable application is in hybrid recommender systems, where attention mechanisms can be used to integrate multiple sources of information. For instance, a hybrid system might combine collaborative filtering and content-based filtering by applying attention mechanisms to weigh the importance of different input features, such as user-item interactions and item attributes. This integration allows the model to dynamically balance the contributions of various information sources, enhancing the robustness and flexibility of the recommendations.

The implications of using attention mechanisms in recommender systems are profound, as they enable the capture of complex, nuanced relationships that traditional methods may miss. By dynamically focusing on the most relevant aspects of the input data, attention-based models can provide more accurate, personalized, and contextually relevant recommendations. However, the implementation of attention mechanisms also presents challenges, including the need for substantial computational resources and the complexity of tuning multiple hyperparameters. Addressing these challenges requires careful model design, efficient training strategies, and continuous evaluation to ensure optimal performance.

In conclusion, attention mechanisms represent a significant advancement in the field of recommender systems, offering powerful tools for capturing intricate dependencies and providing highly personalized recommendations. By dynamically weighting the importance of input features and interactions, attention-based models enhance the flexibility, accuracy, and relevance of recommendations. The successful application of attention mechanisms in various domains, from session-based recommendations to hybrid systems, highlights their transformative potential. As research and development in this area continue to evolve, attention mechanisms will remain at the forefront of innovations in recommender systems, driving improvements in user experience and engagement through more sophisticated and responsive recommendation strategies.

7.3. Reinforcement Learning

Reinforcement learning (RL) has emerged as a powerful paradigm in the development of recommender systems, offering a framework for making sequential decisions that optimize long-term user engagement and satisfaction. Unlike traditional recommendation techniques that typically focus on immediate relevance, RL-based approaches model the recommendation process as a series of interactions between the user and the system, where each recommendation influences future interactions and preferences. This dynamic and adaptive nature of RL makes it particularly well-suited for applications where the goal is to maximize cumulative reward over time, such as maintaining user engagement, improving retention, and enhancing user satisfaction.

At its core, reinforcement learning involves an agent that learns to make decisions by interacting with an environment. The agent receives feedback in the form of rewards or penalties based on the outcomes of its actions, which it uses to refine its decision-making policy. In the context of recommender systems, the agent represents the recommendation algorithm, the environment includes the user and the available items, and the actions correspond to the recommendations made to the user. The objective is to learn a policy that maximizes the expected cumulative reward, which could be defined in terms of user engagement metrics such as click-through rates, dwell time, or conversion rates.

The fundamental components of reinforcement learning include the state space, action space, and reward function. The state space represents the various contexts or situations the system might encounter, encompassing user attributes, interaction history, and contextual factors such as time of day or device type. The action space consists of the possible recommendations that can be made, which could include items, content, or advertisements. The reward function quantifies the immediate benefit of an action, providing the feedback necessary for the agent to learn and improve its policy.

One of the most commonly used algorithms in reinforcement learning is Q-learning, a model-free method that seeks to learn the optimal action-value function $Q(s, a)$. The Q-function represents the expected cumulative reward of taking action a in state s and following the optimal policy thereafter. The Q-learning algorithm updates the Q-values iteratively using the Bellman equation:

$$Q(s, a) \leftarrow Q(s, a) + \alpha \left[r + \gamma \max_{a'} Q(s', a') - Q(s, a) \right]$$

where α is the learning rate, r is the reward received after taking action a in state s, γ is the discount factor that accounts for future rewards, and s' is the subsequent state. Over time, the Q-values converge to the optimal action-value function, enabling the agent to make decisions that maximize long-term rewards.

In recommender systems, deep reinforcement learning (DRL) extends traditional RL by incorporating deep neural networks to approximate the Q-function, allowing the agent to handle high-dimensional state and action spaces. Deep Q-networks (DQNs), for instance, use neural networks to estimate the Q-values, enabling the agent to learn complex policies from raw input data. This approach has proven effective in various recommendation scenarios, where the state space includes user interaction history and item features, and the action space consists of the items to be recommended.

An illustrative application of reinforcement learning in recommender systems is personalized content recommendation on streaming platforms such as YouTube or Netflix. In this context, the state space includes user attributes, viewing history, and contextual information, while the action space comprises the available videos or shows. The reward function can be defined in terms of user engagement metrics, such as video watch time or frequency of interactions. By continuously learning from user interactions, the RL agent can adapt its recommendations to maximize long-term user engagement, providing a personalized and dynamic viewing experience.

Reinforcement learning also finds applications in optimizing ad placements in online advertising platforms. The objective is to recommend ads that not only maximize immediate click-through rates but also consider long-term user engagement and conversion. The state space includes user demographics, browsing history, and contextual factors, while the action space consists of the available ads. The reward function incorporates both immediate clicks and subsequent conversions, guiding the RL agent to balance short-term gains with long-term value. This approach enhances the effectiveness of ad placements by dynamically adjusting recommendations based on evolving user preferences and behaviors.

Despite its advantages, implementing reinforcement learning in recommender systems presents several challenges. The exploration-exploitation trade-off is a fundamental issue, where the agent must balance exploring new recommendations to discover their potential rewards and exploiting known recommendations that have yielded positive outcomes. This trade-off is critical in ensuring that the agent does not become overly biased towards a subset of recommendations, thereby limiting diversity and novelty. Techniques such as epsilon-greedy policies, where the agent occasionally explores random actions, and Thompson sampling, which uses probabilistic methods to balance exploration and exploitation, are commonly employed to address this challenge.

Another challenge is the computational complexity and scalability of reinforcement learning algorithms, particularly when dealing with large state and action spaces. Training deep reinforcement learning models requires substantial computational resources and efficient algorithms to handle the vast amounts of data involved. Techniques such as experience replay, where past interactions are stored and reused for training, and prioritized experience replay, which prioritizes important interactions, can enhance the efficiency and stability of the learning process.

The dynamic nature of user preferences and the non-stationarity of the environment add further complexity to reinforcement learning in recommender systems. User interests can evolve over time, influenced by various factors such as trends, seasonal changes, and external events. The RL agent must continuously adapt to these changes to maintain the relevance of its recommendations. Online learning techniques, where the model is updated in real-time based on new interactions, and meta-learning approaches, which aim to learn how to learn, can help address this issue by enabling the agent to quickly adapt to evolving user preferences.

In conclusion, reinforcement learning offers a powerful and flexible framework for developing recommender systems that optimize long-term user engagement and satisfaction. By modeling the recommendation process as a sequential decision-making problem, RL-based approaches can capture the dynamic and evolving nature of user preferences, providing highly personalized and adaptive recommendations. The application of deep reinforcement learning further enhances the capability to handle complex and high-dimensional data, enabling the development of sophisticated recommendation strategies. Despite the challenges associated with exploration-exploitation trade-offs, computational complexity, and non-stationarity, ongoing research and advancements in reinforcement learning continue to push the boundaries of what is possible in personalized recommendations. As the field evolves, reinforcement learning will remain a critical component of next-generation recommender systems, driving innovation and improving user experiences in an increasingly data-driven world.

7.4. Scalability and Performance Optimization

The increasing volume and complexity of data in modern recommender systems necessitate sophisticated strategies for scalability and performance optimization. As the number of users and items grows, the computational demands of generating real-time recommendations can become prohibitive. Effective scalability and performance optimization are essential to ensure that recommender systems remain responsive, efficient, and capable of delivering accurate, personalized recommendations in a timely manner. This section explores key methodologies and techniques for achieving scalability and optimizing the performance of recommender systems, drawing on examples and mathematical frameworks to elucidate the underlying principles.

One fundamental approach to scalability is the adoption of distributed computing architectures. Distributed systems leverage multiple processors and storage units to handle large datasets and complex computations, distributing the workload across several nodes to enhance processing speed and efficiency. Frameworks such as Apache Hadoop and Apache Spark provide robust platforms for implementing distributed computing in recommender systems. Apache Spark, in particular, is well-suited for iterative algorithms common in machine learning and data processing, offering in-memory computation capabilities that significantly reduce the latency associated with disk I/O operations.

Parallelization is another crucial strategy for scalability. By decomposing large computational tasks into smaller, independent sub-tasks that can be executed concurrently, parallelization harnesses the power of multiple processors to accelerate the computation. In the context of recommender systems, parallelization can be applied to various stages of the recommendation pipeline, including data preprocessing, feature extraction, model training, and inference. For example, matrix factorization techniques such as Alternating Least Squares (ALS) can be parallelized by distributing the computation of user and item matrices across multiple processors, thereby reducing the overall training time.

Another critical aspect of scalability and performance optimization is the use of efficient data structures and algorithms. Techniques such as approximate nearest neighbor (ANN) search can significantly enhance the performance of similarity-based recommendations. Traditional nearest neighbor search algorithms, which require computing the distance between all pairs of items or users, become infeasible as the dataset size increases. ANN algorithms, such as locality-sensitive hashing (LSH) and k-d trees, provide efficient means of identifying approximate neighbors, reducing the computational complexity while maintaining acceptable accuracy. LSH, for example, hashes input items into buckets such that similar items are more likely to fall into the same bucket, allowing for efficient retrieval of approximate neighbors.

$$\text{LSH}(x) = (h_1(x), h_2(x), \ldots, h_k(x))$$

where h_i are hash functions designed to preserve locality. This approach significantly reduces the number of comparisons needed to find similar items, thereby enhancing the scalability of the recommendation system.

The implementation of online learning algorithms is another pivotal strategy for optimizing performance. Online learning allows the model to be updated incrementally as new data arrives, rather than requiring a complete retraining from scratch. This approach is particularly useful in dynamic environments where user preferences and item characteristics change over time. Algorithms such as stochastic gradient descent (SGD) can be adapted for online learning by updating the model parameters iteratively based on each new interaction. The online version of SGD updates the parameters θ after each interaction (x_t, y_t) as follows:

$$\theta_{t+1} = \theta_t - \eta \nabla L(\theta_t; x_t, y_t)$$

where η is the learning rate and L is the loss function. This incremental update mechanism ensures that the model remains current with the latest data, enhancing its relevance and accuracy while reducing the computational burden of batch retraining.

Cache management and memory optimization also play critical roles in enhancing the performance of recommender systems. Efficient caching strategies can significantly reduce the latency of serving recommendations by storing frequently accessed data in memory. Techniques such as least recently used (LRU) caching, which retains the most recently accessed items in memory, can improve the responsiveness of the system. Memory optimization involves structuring the data and algorithms to minimize memory usage, allowing the system to handle larger datasets within the available resources. For instance, sparse matrix representations can be employed to efficiently store user-item interaction data, reducing memory overhead while maintaining computational efficiency.

Latency reduction is another essential consideration for real-time recommendation systems. Techniques such as pre-computation and indexing can drastically reduce the time required to generate recommendations. Pre-computation involves calculating and storing certain values or intermediate results in advance, which can be quickly retrieved during the recommendation process. For example, pre-computing item similarity matrices or user embeddings allows the system to generate recommendations by simple lookups rather than real-time computations. Indexing structures, such as inverted indices and B-trees, facilitate fast retrieval of relevant data, further reducing latency.

Incorporating machine learning models that balance complexity and efficiency is also vital for scalability. While deep learning models offer powerful capabilities for capturing complex patterns, their computational demands can be prohibitive. Techniques such as model compression, pruning, and quantization can reduce the size and computational requirements of deep learning models without significantly compromising their accuracy. Pruning involves removing redundant or less important weights from the model, while quantization reduces the precision of weights, both leading to more efficient inference.

For example, in a large-scale e-commerce recommendation system, combining distributed computing with parallelized algorithms, efficient data structures, and online learning can create a scalable and responsive recommendation engine. Distributed computing frameworks like Apache Spark can handle the large volumes of user and item data, while parallelization of matrix factorization algorithms ensures that model training and updates are performed efficiently. Implementing ANN search with LSH can expedite similarity computations, and online learning algorithms ensure the model adapts to changing user preferences in real-time. Effective caching and memory optimization strategies minimize latency, and model compression techniques ensure that deep learning models remain efficient without sacrificing performance.

In conclusion, scalability and performance optimization are critical components in the design and implementation of effective recommender systems. By leveraging distributed computing, parallelization, efficient data structures, online learning, cache management, latency reduction techniques, and machine learning model optimization, developers can create systems that handle large-scale data and complex computations efficiently. These strategies ensure that recommender systems remain responsive, accurate, and capable of delivering personalized recommendations in real-time, thereby enhancing user satisfaction and engagement. As the volume and complexity of data continue to grow, ongoing research and innovation in scalability and performance optimization will remain essential to the advancement of recommender system technologies, driving their effectiveness and applicability in an increasingly data-driven world.

7.5. Conclusion

The journey through advanced methodologies for recommender systems, culminating in deep learning, attention mechanisms, reinforcement learning, and strategies for scalability and performance optimization, underscores the transformative potential of these technologies in enhancing personalization and user engagement. These advanced techniques represent the cutting edge of recommendation algorithms, addressing the limitations of traditional methods and providing sophisticated solutions for capturing complex user behaviors and preferences. As the digital landscape continues to evolve, the integration of these methodologies into recommender systems will remain paramount, driving innovation and effectiveness in personalized content delivery.

Deep learning has emerged as a cornerstone in modern recommender systems, offering unparalleled capabilities for learning intricate patterns from vast amounts of data. The application of neural collaborative filtering, convolutional neural networks (CNNs), recurrent neural networks (RNNs), and autoencoders has significantly improved the ability to model user-item interactions and generate highly accurate recommendations. By leveraging deep neural networks, recommender systems can capture non-linear relationships and high-dimensional representations that traditional models might miss, providing a richer and more nuanced understanding of user preferences. For instance, Netflix's implementation of deep learning models has enabled the platform to deliver personalized content that adapts dynamically to user behavior, thereby enhancing viewer engagement and retention.

Attention mechanisms have further revolutionized the field by enabling models to focus selectively on the most relevant parts of the input data. This capability is particularly valuable in scenarios where the importance of different input elements varies contextually. Attention mechanisms facilitate the capture of complex dependencies and interactions, leading to more precise and context-aware recommendations. The integration of self-attention mechanisms, as seen in transformer models, allows for the modeling of long-range dependencies and interactions across entire sequences of user behavior. This advancement has been instrumental in improving the quality of recommendations in domains such as personalized news feeds, where understanding the temporal and contextual relevance of user interactions is crucial.

Reinforcement learning introduces a dynamic and adaptive approach to recommender systems, optimizing long-term user engagement and satisfaction by modeling the recommendation process as a sequential decision-making problem. By continuously learning from user interactions, reinforcement learning algorithms can adapt recommendations to evolving user preferences, ensuring sustained relevance and engagement. Techniques such as Q-learning and deep Q-networks (DQNs) have demonstrated their efficacy in balancing exploration and exploitation, providing a robust framework for developing adaptive and personalized recommender systems. The application of reinforcement learning in environments such as e-commerce and streaming services highlights its potential to enhance user experiences by optimizing for long-term user satisfaction rather than immediate rewards.

Scalability and performance optimization are critical for the practical deployment of recommender systems, especially as the volume of data and the number of users grow exponentially. Distributed computing architectures, parallelization, efficient data structures, and online learning algorithms are essential for handling large-scale data and ensuring real-time responsiveness. Techniques such as approximate nearest neighbor (ANN) search, model compression, and caching strategies play pivotal roles in reducing computational complexity and latency, enabling recommender systems to deliver timely and relevant recommendations. For example, Amazon's recommendation engine leverages these strategies to provide personalized product suggestions to millions of users efficiently, demonstrating the importance of scalability and performance optimization in real-world applications.

The integration of these advanced methodologies into recommender systems has profound implications for both users and businesses. For users, the enhanced personalization and relevance of recommendations lead to improved satisfaction and engagement, fostering a more enjoyable and seamless interaction with digital platforms. For businesses, effective recommender systems drive user retention, increase conversion rates, and generate valuable insights into consumer behavior, ultimately contributing to competitive advantage and revenue growth.

However, the implementation of these advanced techniques also presents challenges that require careful consideration. The computational demands of deep learning and reinforcement learning necessitate substantial resources and expertise, while the complexity of attention mechanisms and scalability strategies requires meticulous design and optimization. Ensuring the interpretability and fairness of recommendations is also critical, as users increasingly seek transparency and ethical considerations in digital services. Addressing these challenges involves continuous research, innovation, and refinement, supported by robust evaluation frameworks and user feedback.

In conclusion, the advanced methodologies explored in this section represent the forefront of recommender system technology, offering powerful tools for capturing complex user behaviors and delivering personalized content. Deep learning, attention mechanisms, reinforcement learning, and scalability optimization each contribute unique strengths, collectively enhancing the capability of recommender systems to provide accurate, relevant, and engaging recommendations. As the field continues to evolve, these technologies will play an increasingly vital role in shaping the future of personalized digital experiences, driving innovation and excellence in recommender system development. Through ongoing exploration and integration of these advanced techniques, developers can create sophisticated, responsive, and user-centric recommender systems that meet the dynamic needs and preferences of users in an ever-expanding digital world.

8. Evaluation Metrics and Techniques

Evaluating recommender systems is a critical aspect of their development, as it ensures that the recommendations are both accurate and relevant to users. Without proper evaluation, even the most sophisticated algorithms can fall short of delivering meaningful results. This chapter explores the various metrics and techniques used to evaluate recommender systems, discussing the importance of each and providing detailed methodologies for their implementation. We will delve into precision, recall, F1-score, Mean Reciprocal Rank (MRR), and other metrics, as well as offline and online evaluation methods such as A/B testing.

8.1. Importance of Evaluation

Evaluation is a cornerstone in the development and deployment of recommender systems, serving as the critical process through which the effectiveness, accuracy, and reliability of these systems are assessed. The importance of evaluation cannot be overstated, as it provides the empirical basis for understanding how well a recommender system performs in practice, guiding iterative improvements and ensuring that the system meets user expectations and business objectives. This section delves into the various dimensions of evaluation, highlighting its significance and exploring the key methodologies employed to assess recommender systems.

The primary purpose of evaluation in recommender systems is to measure their ability to predict user preferences accurately and to deliver relevant and personalized recommendations. This is achieved through a combination of offline and online evaluation techniques, each offering distinct insights into the system's performance. Offline evaluation involves testing the recommender system on historical data, where the ground truth is known, allowing for the computation of various performance metrics. Online evaluation, on the other hand, involves deploying the system in a live environment and measuring its impact on user behavior and engagement through A/B testing and other real-time methods. Both approaches are essential, as they complement each other by providing a comprehensive view of the system's effectiveness in different contexts.

Offline evaluation is typically the first step in assessing a recommender system, as it allows for controlled experiments using historical data. Common metrics used in offline evaluation include precision, recall, F1-score, mean squared error (MSE), and root mean squared error (RMSE). Precision measures the proportion of recommended items that are relevant, while recall assesses the proportion of relevant items that have been recommended. The F1-score, which is the harmonic mean of precision and recall, provides a balanced measure of both metrics. MSE and RMSE evaluate the accuracy of predicted ratings by comparing them with actual ratings, with lower values indicating better performance. These metrics offer valuable insights into the system's predictive power and help identify areas for improvement. For example, a high RMSE might indicate that the model is not capturing user preferences accurately, prompting further refinement of the feature engineering or model selection processes.

$$Precision = \frac{|\{relevant\ items\} \cap \{recommended\ items\}|}{|\{recommended\ items\}|}$$

$$Recall = \frac{|\{relevant\ items\} \cap \{recommended\ items\}|}{|\{relevant\ items\}|}$$

$$F1\text{-}score = 2 \times \frac{Precision \times Recall}{Precision + Recall}$$

$$MSE = \frac{1}{N}\sum_{i=1}^{N}(r_i - \hat{r_i})^2$$

$$RMSE = \sqrt{\frac{1}{N}\sum_{i=1}^{N}(r_i - \hat{r_i})^2}$$

Online evaluation is equally important, as it assesses the system's performance in real-world scenarios, where user behavior and preferences are dynamic and evolving. A/B testing is a widely used technique in online evaluation, involving the comparison of two or more versions of a recommender system to determine which one performs better in terms of user engagement and satisfaction. For example, one group of users might be exposed to the current recommendation algorithm, while another group receives recommendations from a new algorithm. Key performance indicators (KPIs) such as click-through rate (CTR), conversion rate, dwell time, and user retention are monitored to evaluate the impact of the recommendations. A significant improvement in these KPIs for the test group would indicate the superiority of the new algorithm, guiding its adoption and further optimization.

The **diversity and novelty** of recommendations are also critical aspects of evaluation. A system that consistently recommends similar items may achieve high precision but fail to engage users over the long term due to a lack of variety. Evaluating the diversity of recommendations involves measuring the extent to which the recommended items differ from one another, thereby ensuring that users are exposed to a broad range of options. Novelty, on the other hand, assesses the system's ability to recommend items that the user has not previously encountered, enhancing the discovery experience. Metrics such as intra-list diversity and average novelty are used to quantify these aspects, providing a more holistic view of the system's performance.

The **robustness and fairness** of recommender systems are increasingly important considerations in evaluation. Robustness refers to the system's ability to maintain performance under varying conditions, such as changes in user behavior or data distribution. Fairness, meanwhile, addresses the need to ensure that recommendations do not systematically disadvantage certain groups of users. Evaluating fairness involves analyzing the distribution of recommendations across different demographic groups and ensuring that the system does not exhibit biases that could lead to unequal treatment. Techniques such as fairness-aware recommendation algorithms and bias detection metrics are employed to address these concerns, ensuring that the system is both effective and equitable.

In the context of **business objectives**, the evaluation of recommender systems extends beyond technical metrics to include strategic goals such as revenue generation, customer loyalty, and brand engagement. For instance, an e-commerce platform might evaluate the impact of recommendations on sales and average order value, while a streaming service might focus on user retention and subscription renewals. These business-oriented metrics provide a broader perspective on the value of the recommender system, aligning its performance with the overall objectives of the organization.

The continuous nature of evaluation is another key aspect, as recommender systems operate in dynamic environments where user preferences and item availability change over time. This necessitates ongoing monitoring and periodic re-evaluation to ensure that the system adapts to new data and maintains its effectiveness. Techniques such as online learning and adaptive algorithms can help in continuously updating the model based on fresh data, thereby enhancing its relevance and accuracy.

In conclusion, the importance of evaluation in recommender systems cannot be overstated, as it provides the empirical foundation for assessing and improving their performance. Through a combination of offline and online evaluation techniques, diversity and novelty metrics, robustness and fairness considerations, and alignment with business objectives, evaluation ensures that recommender systems deliver accurate, relevant, and personalized recommendations. This iterative process of evaluation and refinement is essential for maintaining the effectiveness and reliability of recommender systems in an ever-changing digital landscape. As the field continues to evolve, innovative evaluation methodologies will play a critical role in advancing the state of the art, ensuring that recommender systems meet the complex and dynamic needs of users and organizations alike.

8.2. Common Metrics

Evaluating the performance of recommender systems is a multifaceted process that relies on a variety of metrics, each designed to measure different aspects of recommendation quality and effectiveness. These metrics provide a quantitative basis for comparing algorithms, diagnosing performance issues, and guiding improvements. Understanding and correctly applying these metrics is crucial for developing recommender systems that deliver accurate, relevant, and personalized recommendations. This section explores the most commonly used evaluation metrics in recommender systems, delving into their definitions, applications, and implications.

One of the foundational metrics in recommender system evaluation is **precision**, which measures the proportion of recommended items that are relevant. Precision is particularly important in scenarios where the cost of presenting irrelevant items to users is high, as it directly reflects the accuracy of the recommendations. Mathematically, precision is defined as:

$$Precision = \frac{|\{relevant\ items\} \cap \{recommended\ items\}|}{|\{recommended\ items\}|}$$

For example, if a system recommends ten movies to a user and six of them are relevant (i.e., the user would like them), the precision is 0.6. High precision indicates that the system is effective at selecting relevant items from the pool of potential recommendations.

Recall complements precision by measuring the proportion of relevant items that have been recommended out of all relevant items available. While precision focuses on the accuracy of the recommendations, recall emphasizes the system's ability to capture all relevant items. Recall is defined as:

$$Recall = \frac{|\{relevant\ items\} \cap \{recommended\ items\}|}{|\{relevant\ items\}|}$$

For instance, if a user likes ten movies, and the system recommends four of these ten, the recall is 0.4. High recall indicates that the system is comprehensive in identifying relevant items, but it must be balanced with precision to ensure that not too many irrelevant items are recommended.

The **F1-score** is a metric that balances precision and recall, providing a single measure that captures both aspects. It is the harmonic mean of precision and recall, giving equal weight to both metrics:

$$F1\text{-}score = 2 \times \frac{Precision \times Recall}{Precision + Recall}$$

The F1-score is particularly useful in scenarios where it is crucial to find a balance between precision and recall, ensuring that the system is both accurate and comprehensive in its recommendations.

Mean Squared Error (MSE) and **Root Mean Squared Error (RMSE)** are widely used metrics for evaluating the accuracy of predicted ratings in recommender systems. MSE measures the average of the squares of the errors, providing a sense of the overall prediction error. RMSE, the square root of MSE, is often preferred because it is in the same units as the ratings, making it more interpretable. These metrics are defined as follows:

$$MSE = \frac{1}{N} \sum_{i=1}^{N} (r_i - \hat{r_i})^2$$

$$RMSE = \sqrt{\frac{1}{N} \sum_{i=1}^{N} (r_i - \hat{r_i})^2}$$

where r_i is the actual rating, $\hat{r}_i$ is the predicted rating, and N is the number of ratings. Low MSE or RMSE values indicate that the predictions are close to the actual ratings, signifying high accuracy.

Mean Absolute Error (MAE) is another metric for evaluating rating prediction accuracy, measuring the average absolute difference between the actual and predicted ratings:

$$MAE = \frac{1}{N} \sum_{i=1}^{N} |r_i - \hat{r_i}|$$

MAE is less sensitive to outliers than MSE and RMSE, providing a robust measure of prediction accuracy.

Normalized Discounted Cumulative Gain (NDCG) is a metric that evaluates the ranking quality of recommendations, considering both the relevance and the position of recommended items. NDCG is particularly useful for systems where the order of recommendations matters, such as search engines and top-N recommendation lists. It is defined as:

$$DCG_p = \sum_{i=1}^{p} \frac{2^{r_i} - 1}{\log_2(i + 1)}$$

$$NDCG_p = \frac{DCG_p}{IDCG_p}$$

where r_i is the relevance score of the item at position i, and IDCG is the ideal DCG, representing the best possible ranking. High NDCG values indicate that relevant items are ranked high in the recommendation list, improving user satisfaction.

Hit Rate is a simple yet effective metric that measures the proportion of users for whom the top-N recommendation list contains at least one relevant item. It is defined as:

$$Hit\ Rate = \frac{Number\ of\ hits}{Total\ number\ of\ users}$$

where a "hit" occurs if at least one relevant item is present in the top-N recommendations for a user. Hit rate provides a straightforward measure of the system's ability to include relevant items in the recommendation list.

Coverage is a metric that evaluates the ability of the recommender system to make recommendations across the entire item catalog. It is defined as the proportion of items that can be recommended to users:

$$Coverage = \frac{|\{recommended\ items\}|}{|\{total\ items\}|}$$

High coverage indicates that the system can recommend a diverse set of items, ensuring that less popular items are also considered.

Diversity and **Novelty** are metrics that assess the variety and uniqueness of the recommendations. Diversity measures how different the recommended items are from each other, enhancing the user's experience by providing a broad range of options. Novelty evaluates the degree to which the recommended items are new or unfamiliar to the user, promoting discovery and exploration. These metrics are essential for maintaining user interest and engagement over time.

In conclusion, common metrics for evaluating recommender systems encompass a wide range of performance aspects, from accuracy and ranking quality to diversity and novelty. Precision, recall, F1-score, MSE, RMSE, MAE, NDCG, hit rate, coverage, diversity, and novelty each provide valuable insights into different dimensions of recommendation quality. These metrics collectively ensure that recommender systems are not only accurate but also comprehensive, engaging, and capable of enhancing user satisfaction. By carefully selecting and balancing these metrics, developers can build recommender systems that meet the complex and dynamic needs of users, driving engagement and achieving business objectives in an increasingly competitive digital landscape.

8.3. Offline Evaluation

Offline evaluation serves as a fundamental process in the assessment of recommender systems, providing a controlled environment to test algorithms using historical data before deployment in live settings. This phase of evaluation is critical for understanding the strengths and limitations of different models, guiding iterative improvements, and ensuring that only the most promising algorithms are considered for online testing. By leveraging offline evaluation, researchers and practitioners can conduct extensive experiments, analyze performance metrics, and make data-driven decisions about model selection and optimization.

The core idea behind offline evaluation is to simulate the recommendation process using a pre-collected dataset, typically consisting of user interactions such as ratings, clicks, purchases, or views. This dataset is divided into training and test sets, where the training set is used to build the model, and the test set is used to evaluate its performance. One common method for partitioning the data is k-fold cross-validation, which involves splitting the dataset into k subsets, training the model on k-1 subsets, and evaluating it on the remaining subset. This process is repeated k times, with each subset serving as the test set once, and the results are averaged to obtain a robust estimate of model performance.

$$CV\ score = \frac{1}{k}\sum_{i=1}^{k} score_i$$

where $score_i$ is the performance metric for the i-th fold.

The choice of performance metrics in offline evaluation is critical, as they provide quantitative measures of how well the model performs. Common metrics such as precision, recall, F1-score, mean squared error (MSE), and root mean squared error (RMSE) offer insights into different aspects of model accuracy and effectiveness. Precision and recall, for instance, measure the relevance of the recommended items, with precision focusing on the proportion of relevant items among the recommended ones, and recall assessing the proportion of relevant items that have been recommended. The F1-score balances these two metrics, providing a single measure that captures both accuracy and completeness.

Mean squared error and root mean squared error evaluate the accuracy of predicted ratings by comparing them with actual ratings. These metrics are particularly useful in rating prediction tasks, where the goal is to estimate the user's rating for an item as accurately as possible. Lower MSE and RMSE values indicate that the predicted ratings are closer to the actual ratings, signifying high accuracy.

$$MSE = \frac{1}{N} \sum_{i=1}^{N} (r_i - \hat{r_i})^2$$

$$RMSE = \sqrt{\frac{1}{N} \sum_{i=1}^{N} (r_i - \hat{r_i})^2}$$

where r_i is the actual rating, $\hat{r_i}$ is the predicted rating, and N is the number of ratings.

Offline evaluation also employs ranking metrics such as Normalized Discounted Cumulative Gain (NDCG) to assess the quality of the recommendation lists. NDCG considers both the relevance and the position of recommended items, providing a measure of ranking quality. High NDCG values indicate that relevant items are ranked higher in the recommendation list, enhancing user satisfaction.

$$DCG_p = \sum_{i=1}^{p} \frac{2^{r_i} - 1}{\log_2(i + 1)}$$

$$NDCG_p = \frac{DCG_p}{IDCG_p}$$

where r_i is the relevance score of the item at position i, and IDCG is the ideal DCG, representing the best possible ranking.

Another important aspect of offline evaluation is the assessment of diversity and novelty in recommendations. These metrics ensure that the recommender system not only provides relevant items but also promotes a broad range of options and introduces users to new and potentially interesting items. Diversity measures the dissimilarity among recommended items, encouraging a varied set of suggestions that can cater to different user preferences. Novelty, on the other hand, evaluates the extent to which the recommended items are new to the user, fostering exploration and discovery.

Offline evaluation also involves **robustness testing**, where the model's performance is assessed under different conditions and perturbations. This includes evaluating the system's resilience to changes in user behavior, data sparsity, and the presence of noise. Robustness metrics help identify potential vulnerabilities and ensure that the recommender system maintains its effectiveness even when confronted with unforeseen challenges.

Moreover, offline evaluation facilitates the exploration of **different algorithms and configurations** without the risks and costs associated with live deployment. Researchers can experiment with various model architectures, hyperparameters, and feature engineering techniques to identify the most effective combinations. This process of experimentation and optimization is crucial for developing high-performing recommender systems that are well-suited to the specific characteristics of the data and the objectives of the application.

The implications of thorough offline evaluation are significant. It allows for the identification of the best-performing models, ensuring that only the most promising algorithms are advanced to the online evaluation phase. By rigorously testing models in a controlled environment, offline evaluation helps prevent the deployment of suboptimal systems, reducing the risk of negatively impacting user experience and engagement. Additionally, it provides valuable insights into the strengths and weaknesses of different approaches, guiding future research and development efforts.

However, it is important to acknowledge the limitations of offline evaluation. While it provides a useful approximation of real-world performance, it cannot fully capture the dynamic and interactive nature of user behavior. Users' responses to recommendations can vary based on numerous contextual factors that are difficult to replicate in an offline setting. Therefore, offline evaluation should be complemented with online testing to obtain a comprehensive understanding of the system's effectiveness.

In conclusion, offline evaluation is a critical component of the recommender system development process, offering a structured and empirical approach to assessing model performance. By employing a variety of metrics and methodologies, offline evaluation provides a robust framework for identifying high-performing models and guiding iterative improvements. Despite its limitations, it plays an indispensable role in ensuring that recommender systems are accurate, effective, and ready for deployment in real-world environments. As the field continues to evolve, advancements in offline evaluation techniques will further enhance our ability to build sophisticated and reliable recommender systems that meet the complex needs of users and businesses alike.

8.4. Online Evaluation

Online evaluation represents the culmination of the recommender system development process, where the system is tested and refined in a live environment with real users. Unlike offline evaluation, which relies on historical data, online evaluation provides direct insights into how users interact with the system in real-time, capturing the dynamic and contextual nuances of user behavior. This phase is crucial for validating the practical effectiveness of the recommender system, ensuring that it meets user expectations and achieves business objectives. Through various techniques such as A/B testing, interleaving, and multi-armed bandits, online evaluation offers a comprehensive framework for assessing the impact of recommendations on user engagement and satisfaction.

A/B testing is one of the most widely used methods in online evaluation. It involves comparing the performance of two or more versions of a recommender system by exposing different user groups to each version and measuring key performance indicators (KPIs). For example, one group of users (the control group) might receive recommendations from the current system, while another group (the treatment group) receives recommendations from a new algorithm. By monitoring metrics such as click-through rate (CTR), conversion rate, dwell time, and user retention, A/B testing provides a clear and quantitative assessment of the relative performance of the different systems. The statistical rigor of A/B testing ensures that observed differences in performance are attributable to the changes in the recommendation algorithm, rather than random variation.

$$CTR = \frac{Number\ of\ clicks}{Number\ of\ impressions}$$

$$Conversion\ Rate = \frac{Number\ of\ conversions}{Number\ of\ visitors}$$

Interleaving is another technique used in online evaluation, particularly suited for comparing ranking algorithms. In interleaving, recommendations from multiple algorithms are combined into a single ranked list, and user interactions with this list are monitored to infer preferences. This method allows for a more granular comparison of algorithms, as it provides insights into the relative performance of each algorithm within the same session. Interleaving can be especially useful when incremental changes to ranking algorithms are tested, as it minimizes the risk of user disruption by blending the new recommendations with the existing ones.

Multi-armed bandits offer a sophisticated approach to online evaluation, balancing the exploration of new algorithms with the exploitation of known effective ones. Multi-armed bandit algorithms dynamically adjust the allocation of user traffic to different versions of the recommender system based on their performance. This approach is particularly advantageous in fast-paced environments where continuous improvement is necessary, as it allows for rapid identification and adoption of superior algorithms while minimizing the opportunity cost of exploration.

The primary advantage of online evaluation is its ability to capture real-time user feedback, providing a direct measure of how well the recommender system performs in a live setting. This feedback loop is essential for iterative improvement, as it highlights the practical effectiveness of the recommendations and identifies areas for refinement. For instance, if an online evaluation reveals that a new algorithm significantly increases the CTR but decreases user retention, this insight can guide further optimization to balance short-term engagement with long-term satisfaction.

Contextual factors play a critical role in online evaluation, as user preferences and behaviors can vary significantly based on context. Factors such as time of day, device type, location, and user activity can influence the relevance and effectiveness of recommendations. Online evaluation allows for the analysis of these contextual variables, enabling the development of context-aware recommender systems that adapt to the specific circumstances of each user interaction. By incorporating contextual data into the evaluation process, developers can ensure that the recommendations are not only accurate but also timely and appropriate for the user's current situation.

The implications of online evaluation extend beyond technical performance metrics to encompass user experience and business outcomes. High-performing recommender systems enhance user satisfaction by delivering relevant and engaging recommendations, fostering increased engagement and loyalty. From a business perspective, effective recommendations can drive revenue growth by boosting conversion rates, increasing average order value, and reducing churn. Therefore, online evaluation is not only a tool for technical validation but also a strategic instrument for achieving business objectives.

Challenges in online evaluation include ensuring the ethical use of user data and maintaining user trust. Given the real-time nature of online evaluation, it is essential to implement robust privacy protections and transparent communication with users about how their data is being used. Ensuring that the evaluation process does not negatively impact user experience is also critical, as poorly performing algorithms or frequent changes can lead to user dissatisfaction. Balancing the need for experimentation with the imperative to provide a consistent and positive user experience is a key consideration in the design of online evaluation strategies.

In conclusion, online evaluation is a vital component of the recommender system lifecycle, providing a real-world assessment of system performance and user impact. Techniques such as A/B testing, interleaving, and multi-armed bandits offer powerful methodologies for comparing algorithms, capturing user feedback, and driving iterative improvements. By considering contextual factors and aligning evaluation metrics with business objectives, online evaluation ensures that recommender systems are both effective and strategically valuable. The insights gained from online evaluation guide the continuous refinement of recommendation algorithms, enhancing their ability to deliver personalized, relevant, and engaging experiences to users. As the digital landscape evolves, the importance of rigorous and ethical online evaluation will continue to grow, ensuring that recommender systems remain at the forefront of personalization technologies.

8.5. Interpreting Results

Interpreting the results of recommender system evaluations is a nuanced process that requires a deep understanding of the underlying metrics, the context in which the system operates, and the broader implications of the findings. The goal is not only to determine whether a particular algorithm or model performs well according to specific metrics but also to understand why it performs as it does and how these results can be used to drive further improvements and strategic decisions. This section delves into the principles and practices of interpreting evaluation results, providing a comprehensive framework for making sense of the data and translating it into actionable insights.

The first step in interpreting results is to understand the **performance metrics** in detail. Metrics such as precision, recall, F1-score, MSE, RMSE, NDCG, hit rate, and others provide quantitative measures of different aspects of recommendation quality. Each metric offers a unique perspective on performance, and understanding the trade-offs between them is crucial. For instance, high precision indicates that the recommended items are relevant, but if recall is low, it suggests that many relevant items are being missed. The F1-score, which balances precision and recall, can provide a more holistic view, but it is essential to consider the specific goals of the recommender system. For example, in a streaming service, recall might be more critical to ensure users discover a broad range of content, whereas in an e-commerce platform, precision might be prioritized to drive immediate conversions.

$$F1\text{-}score = 2 \times \frac{Precision \times Recall}{Precision + Recall}$$

Understanding the context in which the recommender system operates is also vital. User behavior and preferences can vary widely across different domains and use cases, affecting how the results should be interpreted. For instance, the same level of performance might be considered exceptional in one context but merely adequate in another. Consider the difference between a news recommendation system and a music recommendation system: users might expect high novelty in news recommendations to stay informed about current events, whereas they might prefer familiar and highly personalized music recommendations. Thus, interpreting results requires a keen awareness of the user expectations and business objectives specific to the domain.

Analyzing the distribution of performance across different user segments can reveal important insights that are not apparent from aggregate metrics alone. Recommender systems often exhibit varying performance for different user groups, such as new versus long-term users, active versus inactive users, or users with diverse tastes versus those with more specific preferences. By segmenting the user base and evaluating the performance within each segment, it is possible to identify patterns and potential areas for improvement. For example, if a system performs well for active users but poorly for new users, targeted interventions such as onboarding improvements or cold start strategies might be necessary.

The **explanation of results** is another crucial aspect of interpretation. Beyond understanding the numerical metrics, it is important to delve into the reasons behind the performance of the recommender system. Techniques such as feature importance analysis, model interpretability methods, and error analysis can provide insights into why certain recommendations are made and why certain errors occur. For instance, feature importance analysis can highlight which user or item attributes are most influential in the recommendation process, guiding further refinement of feature engineering. Similarly, analyzing the errors where the system failed to provide relevant recommendations can uncover gaps in the data or model assumptions that need to be addressed.

Contextual factors also play a significant role in interpreting results. The performance of a recommender system can be influenced by various contextual variables such as time of day, location, device type, and user activity. By incorporating contextual information into the evaluation and interpretation process, it is possible to gain a more nuanced understanding of the system's effectiveness. For instance, a recommender system might perform differently during peak hours compared to off-peak hours, or on mobile devices versus desktop computers. Understanding these contextual variations can help in tailoring the recommendations to better suit the specific circumstances of each user interaction.

Comparative analysis is another valuable tool for interpreting results. By comparing the performance of different algorithms or models under the same conditions, it is possible to identify the strengths and weaknesses of each approach. This comparison can be done using statistical tests to determine whether observed differences in performance are statistically significant. Techniques such as paired t-tests or Wilcoxon signed-rank tests can provide rigorous evidence of whether one model consistently outperforms another. For example, if two algorithms are compared using a paired t-test on their precision scores across multiple datasets, a significant result would indicate that the observed differences are unlikely to be due to chance.

$$t = \frac{\bar{d}}{s_d/\sqrt{n}}$$

where $\bar{d}$ is the mean difference between paired observations, s_d is the standard deviation of the differences, and n is the number of pairs.

The **implications of the findings** extend beyond the immediate performance metrics to strategic decisions and future directions. Effective interpretation involves considering how the results can inform broader business strategies and user engagement efforts. For example, if a recommender system significantly increases user engagement but has a minor impact on conversions, the results might suggest focusing on enhancing the user experience to build long-term loyalty, while also exploring ways to nudge users towards higher-value actions. The findings can also guide the allocation of resources for further development, highlighting areas where additional data collection, feature engineering, or algorithm refinement is needed.

Visualizing results can greatly aid in their interpretation, making complex data more accessible and understandable. Visualization tools such as precision-recall curves, ROC curves, and heatmaps can provide intuitive representations of performance metrics, helping stakeholders grasp the implications of the results more easily. For instance, a precision-recall curve can illustrate the trade-off between precision and recall at different thresholds, providing a clear visual representation of how changes in the recommendation threshold affect performance.

In conclusion, interpreting the results of recommender system evaluations is a complex and multifaceted task that requires a deep understanding of performance metrics, contextual factors, user behavior, and business objectives. By carefully analyzing the data, explaining the underlying reasons for observed performance, and considering the broader implications of the findings, practitioners can derive meaningful insights that drive the continuous improvement of recommender systems. Effective interpretation not only ensures that the system performs well according to quantitative metrics but also aligns with user expectations and strategic goals, ultimately enhancing the value and impact of the recommendations in real-world applications.

8.6. Conclusion

The rigorous evaluation of recommender systems is essential to ensuring their effectiveness, relevance, and fairness in various applications. Throughout our exploration of evaluation metrics and techniques, we have highlighted the critical role these tools play in assessing and optimizing the performance of recommendation algorithms. The multifaceted nature of recommender systems necessitates a comprehensive evaluation framework that incorporates both quantitative and qualitative measures. This section synthesizes the key insights and implications derived from the detailed examination of evaluation metrics and techniques, emphasizing their importance in the development and deployment of robust recommender systems.

Evaluation metrics provide a quantitative basis for assessing the accuracy, relevance, and utility of recommendations. Traditional metrics such as precision, recall, and F1-score measure the ability of the system to deliver relevant items to users, focusing on the trade-off between the number of relevant recommendations retrieved and the total number of recommendations made. Precision, defined as the ratio of relevant items to the total recommended items, and recall, the ratio of relevant items retrieved to the total relevant items available, offer insights into the effectiveness of the recommendation algorithm. The F1-score, which combines precision and recall into a single metric, provides a balanced measure of the system's performance.

In addition to these traditional metrics, advanced metrics such as Mean Squared Error (MSE), Root Mean Squared Error (RMSE), and Normalized Discounted Cumulative Gain (NDCG) offer deeper insights into the quality of recommendations. MSE and RMSE evaluate the accuracy of predicted ratings by comparing them to actual user ratings, with lower values indicating better predictive accuracy. NDCG, on the other hand, assesses the ranking quality of recommendations by considering the position of relevant items in the recommendation list. This metric is particularly useful in scenarios where the order of recommendations significantly impacts user satisfaction, such as in search engine results or content feeds.

The application of these metrics in offline evaluation provides a controlled environment for testing and refining recommendation algorithms. Offline evaluation uses historical data to simulate user interactions and assess the performance of different models. This approach allows developers to compare various algorithms, fine-tune hyperparameters, and identify the most promising models before deploying them in a live environment. However, offline evaluation has limitations, as it cannot fully capture the dynamic nature of user behavior and the real-time impact of recommendations.

Online evaluation techniques, such as A/B testing, interleaving, and multi-armed bandits, complement offline evaluation by providing real-time insights into user engagement and satisfaction. A/B testing involves comparing the performance of different recommendation algorithms by exposing different user groups to different versions of the system. This technique provides direct feedback on the impact of recommendations on user behavior, such as click-through rates, conversion rates, and dwell time. Interleaving, which involves mixing recommendations from different algorithms in a single list, allows for a more granular comparison of their performance. Multi-armed bandits, which dynamically allocate traffic to different algorithms based on their real-time performance, offer an adaptive approach to online evaluation, optimizing for user engagement and satisfaction while minimizing the risk of poor recommendations.

The interpretation of evaluation results is a nuanced process that extends beyond numerical metrics. It involves understanding the broader context and implications of the findings, such as the trade-offs between different metrics and the impact on user experience. For example, a high precision score might indicate accurate recommendations, but if recall is low, the system may be missing many relevant items, suggesting a need for further optimization. Similarly, variations in performance across user segments can reveal specific areas for improvement, such as addressing the cold start problem for new users or enhancing recommendations for users with diverse tastes.

Furthermore, evaluating the fairness and transparency of recommender systems is crucial for ensuring ethical and responsible deployment. Fairness-aware metrics and bias detection tools help identify and mitigate biases in recommendations, ensuring that the system treats all user groups equitably. Transparency mechanisms, such as explainable AI techniques, provide users with insights into the recommendation process, fostering trust and accountability. These ethical considerations are integral to the comprehensive evaluation of recommender systems, aligning technical performance with societal values.

In conclusion, the evaluation of recommender systems is a multifaceted and dynamic process that is essential for their success. A comprehensive evaluation framework that incorporates both offline and online techniques, quantitative and qualitative metrics, and ethical considerations provides a robust basis for assessing and optimizing the performance of recommendation algorithms. By continuously evaluating and refining recommender systems, we can ensure that they deliver accurate, relevant, and personalized recommendations that enhance user satisfaction and drive business success. The insights gained from rigorous evaluation not only inform the development of more effective algorithms but also guide the responsible deployment of recommender systems, ensuring that they align with user needs and societal values. As the field continues to advance, ongoing research and innovation in evaluation techniques will be crucial for maintaining the effectiveness and ethical integrity of recommender systems in an ever-evolving digital landscape.

9. Case Studies and Practical Applications

Recommender systems have become integral to a wide array of industries, driving engagement, satisfaction, and revenue by delivering personalized content and product suggestions. This chapter delves into real-world case studies that illustrate the practical applications of recommender systems across different domains, highlighting the challenges faced, solutions implemented, and outcomes achieved. By examining these examples, you will gain valuable insights and best practices that can be applied to your own projects.

9.1. Case Study 1: E-commerce Personalization

E-commerce personalization represents one of the most significant applications of recommender systems, fundamentally transforming how consumers interact with online retail platforms. This case study examines the implementation and impact of personalized recommendations within an e-commerce context, highlighting the methodologies used, the challenges encountered, and the outcomes achieved. By delving into the intricacies of an e-commerce personalization system, we can elucidate the critical role of recommendation algorithms in enhancing user experience, increasing engagement, and driving sales.

In an e-commerce environment, the vast array of products available poses a challenge for consumers who must sift through numerous items to find those that meet their preferences and needs. Personalized recommendation systems address this challenge by leveraging data on user behavior, preferences, and interactions to suggest products that are most likely to interest individual users. The primary objective is to create a tailored shopping experience that enhances user satisfaction and increases the likelihood of purchase.

The foundation of e-commerce personalization lies in the collection and analysis of user data. This data encompasses explicit feedback, such as product ratings and reviews, and implicit feedback, such as click-through rates, browsing history, and purchase behavior. By integrating these diverse data sources, the recommendation system constructs comprehensive user profiles that capture individual preferences and behaviors. For example, a user who frequently browses and purchases electronic gadgets will have a profile that reflects this interest, guiding the recommendation system to suggest similar products or complementary items.

Collaborative filtering and content-based filtering are two primary algorithms employed in e-commerce personalization. Collaborative filtering leverages the collective behavior of users to identify patterns and similarities. In user-based collaborative filtering, the algorithm identifies users with similar preferences and recommends products that these similar users have liked. Mathematically, the similarity between users u and v can be calculated using cosine similarity:

$$sim(u, v) = \frac{\sum_{i \in I_{uv}} r_{ui} r_{vi}}{\sqrt{\sum_{i \in I_u} r_{ui}^2} \sqrt{\sum_{i \in I_v} r_{vi}^2}}$$

where I_{uv} is the set of items rated by both users, and r_{ui} and r_{vi} are the ratings given by users u and v, respectively. Item-based collaborative filtering, on the other hand, focuses on the similarities between items and recommends products that are similar to those the user has interacted with. This approach is particularly effective in identifying complementary products, such as recommending a phone case to someone who has purchased a smartphone.

Content-based filtering, in contrast, uses the attributes of items to recommend products similar to those the user has previously liked. This involves analyzing product features, such as category, brand, price, and specifications, and matching them with the user's profile. For instance, if a user has shown a preference for a particular brand of clothing, the system can recommend other items from the same brand. The effectiveness of content-based filtering relies on the richness and accuracy of the product attributes, as well as the system's ability to model user preferences accurately.

Hybrid recommender systems combine collaborative and content-based filtering to leverage the strengths of both approaches while mitigating their respective weaknesses. For example, a hybrid system might use collaborative filtering to generate an initial list of product recommendations and then refine this list using content-based filtering to ensure the recommendations are aligned with the user's specific preferences. This integrated approach enhances the robustness and accuracy of the recommendations, providing a more personalized shopping experience.

The implementation of a personalized recommendation system in e-commerce also involves addressing challenges such as the cold start problem, data sparsity, and scalability. The cold start problem occurs when there is insufficient data about new users or products, making it difficult to generate accurate recommendations. This issue can be mitigated by incorporating content-based features and using hybrid methods that do not rely solely on user interaction data. Data sparsity, where the user-item interaction matrix is predominantly empty, is another common challenge. Techniques such as matrix factorization and imputation methods help address this by uncovering latent factors and filling in missing values.

Scalability is a critical consideration in e-commerce personalization, given the large number of users and products involved. Efficient algorithms and data structures are essential to ensure that the recommendation system can handle the scale and deliver real-time recommendations. Distributed computing frameworks, parallel processing, and optimization techniques such as Approximate Nearest Neighbors (ANN) search are employed to enhance scalability and performance.

The impact of personalized recommendations on e-commerce platforms is profound. Personalized recommendations drive user engagement by presenting relevant products that align with individual preferences, reducing the effort required to find desirable items. This increased engagement translates into higher conversion rates, as users are more likely to purchase products that are tailored to their tastes. Additionally, personalized recommendations contribute to higher average order values by suggesting complementary products and upsell opportunities. For example, recommending accessories alongside a main product can encourage users to make additional purchases, boosting overall sales.

Empirical studies and real-world implementations have demonstrated the effectiveness of personalized recommendation systems in e-commerce. Companies like Amazon, Netflix, and Alibaba have leveraged these systems to enhance user experience and drive significant revenue growth. Amazon's recommendation engine, for instance, accounts for a substantial portion of its sales by suggesting products based on users' browsing and purchasing history. The success of these systems underscores the value of personalization in creating a competitive advantage in the e-commerce landscape.

In conclusion, e-commerce personalization through recommender systems is a powerful tool that enhances user experience, increases engagement, and drives sales. By leveraging collaborative filtering, content-based filtering, and hybrid approaches, these systems provide tailored product recommendations that align with individual preferences. The implementation of personalized recommendation systems involves addressing challenges such as the cold start problem, data sparsity, and scalability, ensuring that the system can deliver accurate and timely recommendations. The impact of personalized recommendations on e-commerce platforms is significant, leading to higher conversion rates, increased average order values, and improved user satisfaction. As e-commerce continues to evolve, the role of personalization in shaping the future of online retail will only become more critical, underscoring the importance of ongoing innovation and refinement in recommender system technologies.

9.2. Case Study 2: Media and Entertainment Recommendations

In the realm of media and entertainment, personalized recommendations have revolutionized how audiences discover content, enhancing user experience and driving engagement. This case study explores the implementation and impact of recommendation systems in media and entertainment, detailing the methodologies employed, the challenges encountered, and the outcomes achieved. By analyzing the intricacies of media recommendation systems, we can elucidate the significant role they play in shaping user preferences and sustaining viewer loyalty in an increasingly competitive landscape.

The media and entertainment industry encompasses a diverse array of content types, including movies, TV shows, music, podcasts, and articles. Personalized recommendation systems leverage user data to tailor content suggestions, ensuring that each user receives recommendations aligned with their unique tastes and preferences. The primary objective is to facilitate content discovery, thereby increasing user satisfaction and engagement while reducing churn rates.

At the core of media recommendation systems lies the collection and analysis of extensive user data. This data includes explicit feedback, such as ratings, likes, and comments, as well as implicit feedback, such as viewing history, listening patterns, and interaction durations. By integrating these data sources, the recommendation system constructs detailed user profiles that capture individual preferences and behaviors. For example, a user who frequently watches science fiction movies and listens to electronic music will have a profile reflecting these interests, guiding the recommendation system to suggest similar content.

Collaborative filtering and content-based filtering are the foundational algorithms used in media recommendation systems. Collaborative filtering, particularly matrix factorization techniques, excels in identifying patterns in user behavior and leveraging them to predict future preferences. In user-based collaborative filtering, the system identifies users with similar viewing or listening habits and recommends content that these similar users have enjoyed. Mathematically, the similarity between users u and v can be computed using Pearson correlation:

$$sim(u, v) = \frac{\sum_{i \in I_{uv}} (r_{ui} - \bar{r_u})(r_{vi} - \bar{r_v})}{\sqrt{\sum_{i \in I_u} (r_{ui} - \bar{r_u})^2} \sqrt{\sum_{i \in I_v} (r_{vi} - \bar{r_v})^2}}$$

where I_{uv} is the set of items rated by both users, and r_{ui} and r_{vi} are the ratings given by users u and v, respectively, with $\bar{r_u}$ and $\bar{r_v}$ representing their mean ratings. Item-based collaborative filtering, on the other hand, recommends content similar to items the user has already interacted with, such as suggesting TV shows similar to those previously watched.

Content-based filtering, in contrast, focuses on the attributes of the content itself to make recommendations. This involves analyzing features such as genre, director, cast, and keywords for movies and TV shows, or genre, artist, and tempo for music. For instance, if a user frequently watches thriller movies directed by a particular filmmaker, the system can recommend other thrillers by the same director or with similar thematic elements. The effectiveness of content-based filtering depends on the richness and granularity of the content metadata and the system's ability to accurately model user preferences based on these features.

Hybrid recommendation systems combine collaborative and content-based filtering to leverage their respective strengths while mitigating their weaknesses. For example, a hybrid system might use collaborative filtering to generate an initial list of recommendations and then apply content-based filtering to refine this list, ensuring the suggestions are highly relevant to the user's specific interests. This approach enhances the robustness and accuracy of the recommendations, providing a more comprehensive and personalized content discovery experience.

Implementing personalized recommendation systems in media and entertainment also involves addressing challenges such as the cold start problem, data sparsity, and scalability. The cold start problem arises when there is insufficient data about new users or new content, making it difficult to generate accurate recommendations. This issue can be mitigated by leveraging content-based features and using hybrid methods that do not rely solely on user interaction data. Data sparsity, where the user-item interaction matrix is predominantly empty, is another common challenge. Techniques such as matrix factorization and imputation methods help address this by uncovering latent factors and filling in missing values.

Scalability is a critical consideration in media recommendation systems, given the vast number of users and the extensive catalog of content. Efficient algorithms and data structures are essential to ensure the system can handle the scale and deliver real-time recommendations. Distributed computing frameworks, parallel processing, and optimization techniques such as Approximate Nearest Neighbors (ANN) search are employed to enhance scalability and performance.

The impact of personalized recommendations in media and entertainment is substantial. Personalized recommendations drive user engagement by presenting content that aligns with individual preferences, reducing the effort required to find desirable content. This increased engagement translates into higher retention rates, as users are more likely to continue using a service that consistently provides relevant and enjoyable recommendations. Additionally, personalized recommendations contribute to higher content consumption, as users are encouraged to explore new content that matches their tastes. For example, recommending similar TV shows or suggesting new artists based on listening habits can lead to increased viewing and listening time, enhancing overall user satisfaction.

Empirical studies and real-world implementations have demonstrated the effectiveness of personalized recommendation systems in media and entertainment. Companies like Netflix, Spotify, and YouTube have leveraged these systems to enhance user experience and drive significant engagement and revenue growth. Netflix's recommendation engine, for instance, plays a crucial role in user retention by suggesting movies and TV shows based on viewing history and user ratings. Spotify's Discover Weekly playlist uses collaborative filtering and natural language processing to recommend personalized music selections, fostering user loyalty and discovery. The success of these systems underscores the value of personalization in creating a competitive advantage in the media and entertainment industry.

In conclusion, media and entertainment recommendation systems are powerful tools that enhance user experience, increase engagement, and drive content consumption. By leveraging collaborative filtering, content-based filtering, and hybrid approaches, these systems provide tailored content recommendations that align with individual preferences. The implementation of personalized recommendation systems involves addressing challenges such as the cold start problem, data sparsity, and scalability, ensuring that the system can deliver accurate and timely recommendations. The impact of personalized recommendations on media and entertainment platforms is significant, leading to higher retention rates, increased content consumption, and improved user satisfaction. As the media and entertainment industry continues to evolve, the role of personalization in shaping the future of content discovery will only become more critical, underscoring the importance of ongoing innovation and refinement in recommender system technologies.

9.3. Case Study 3: Social Media Content Suggestions

In the dynamic and fast-paced world of social media, personalized content suggestions have become indispensable for enhancing user engagement and satisfaction. This case study explores the implementation and impact of recommendation systems within social media platforms, elucidating the methodologies used, the challenges encountered, and the outcomes achieved. By examining the intricacies of social media content recommendation systems, we can understand their pivotal role in shaping user experiences, increasing engagement, and fostering community interactions.

Social media platforms generate a vast amount of user-generated content daily, including posts, images, videos, and comments. Personalized content suggestion systems leverage this wealth of data to provide users with relevant and engaging content, tailored to their individual preferences and interactions. The primary goal is to ensure that each user receives content that is interesting, timely, and contextually relevant, thereby enhancing their overall experience on the platform.

The foundation of social media content suggestion systems lies in the collection and analysis of user data. This data includes explicit feedback, such as likes, shares, comments, and follows, as well as implicit feedback, such as viewing duration, click-through rates, and browsing history. By integrating these diverse data sources, the recommendation system constructs detailed user profiles that capture individual preferences, behaviors, and social connections. For instance, a user who frequently engages with technology news and follows tech influencers will have a profile reflecting these interests, guiding the recommendation system to suggest similar content.

Collaborative filtering and **content-based filtering** are the primary algorithms employed in social media content suggestion systems. Collaborative filtering leverages the behavior of similar users to make recommendations. In user-based collaborative filtering, the system identifies users with similar interaction patterns and recommends content that these similar users have engaged with. Mathematically, the similarity between users u and v can be computed using the cosine similarity:

$$sim(u, v) = \frac{\sum_{i \in I_{uv}} r_{ui} r_{vi}}{\sqrt{\sum_{i \in I_u} r_{ui}^2} \sqrt{\sum_{i \in I_v} r_{vi}^2}}$$

where I_{uv} is the set of items interacted with by both users, and r_{ui} and r_{vi} are the interaction strengths of users u and v, respectively. Item-based collaborative filtering, on the other hand, recommends content similar to items the user has previously interacted with, such as suggesting posts similar to those a user has liked or shared.

Content-based filtering focuses on the attributes of the content itself to make recommendations. This involves analyzing features such as hashtags, keywords, content type, and the presence of multimedia elements. For example, if a user frequently engages with posts tagged with #Travel and #Adventure, the system can recommend other posts with similar tags or content. The effectiveness of content-based filtering relies on the richness and granularity of the content metadata and the system's ability to accurately model user preferences based on these features.

Hybrid recommendation systems combine collaborative and content-based filtering to leverage their respective strengths while mitigating their weaknesses. For example, a hybrid system might use collaborative filtering to generate an initial list of recommended posts and then apply content-based filtering to refine this list, ensuring that the suggestions are highly relevant to the user's specific interests. This integrated approach enhances the robustness and accuracy of the recommendations, providing a more personalized content discovery experience.

Implementing personalized content suggestion systems in social media involves addressing challenges such as the cold start problem, data sparsity, and scalability. The cold start problem arises when there is insufficient data about new users or new content, making it difficult to generate accurate recommendations. This issue can be mitigated by leveraging content-based features and using hybrid methods that do not rely solely on user interaction data. Data sparsity, where the user-item interaction matrix is predominantly empty, is another common challenge. Techniques such as matrix factorization and imputation methods help address this by uncovering latent factors and filling in missing values.

Scalability is a critical consideration in social media content suggestion systems, given the vast number of users and the extensive volume of content generated daily. Efficient algorithms and data structures are essential to ensure that the system can handle the scale and deliver real-time recommendations. Distributed computing frameworks, parallel processing, and optimization techniques such as Approximate Nearest Neighbors (ANN) search are employed to enhance scalability and performance.

The impact of personalized content suggestions on social media platforms is profound. Personalized recommendations drive user engagement by presenting content that aligns with individual preferences, reducing the effort required to find interesting content. This increased engagement translates into higher retention rates, as users are more likely to continue using a platform that consistently provides relevant and enjoyable content. Additionally, personalized content suggestions contribute to higher interaction rates, as users are encouraged to like, share, comment, and engage with content that resonates with them. For example, suggesting relevant articles, trending videos, or popular posts based on a user's interaction history can lead to increased content consumption and deeper engagement.

Empirical studies and real-world implementations have demonstrated the effectiveness of personalized content suggestion systems in social media. Platforms like Facebook, Twitter, and Instagram have leveraged these systems to enhance user experience and drive significant engagement and growth. Facebook's News Feed algorithm, for instance, uses collaborative filtering, content-based filtering, and machine learning techniques to prioritize posts that are most likely to interest individual users. Twitter's recommendation system suggests tweets, accounts to follow, and trending topics based on user interactions and preferences. Instagram's Explore feature uses similar techniques to recommend photos and videos tailored to each user's interests. The success of these systems underscores the value of personalization in creating a competitive advantage in the social media landscape.

In conclusion, social media content suggestion systems are powerful tools that enhance user experience, increase engagement, and foster community interactions. By leveraging collaborative filtering, content-based filtering, and hybrid approaches, these systems provide tailored content recommendations that align with individual preferences. The implementation of personalized content suggestion systems involves addressing challenges such as the cold start problem, data sparsity, and scalability, ensuring that the system can deliver accurate and timely recommendations. The impact of personalized content suggestions on social media platforms is significant, leading to higher retention rates, increased interaction rates, and improved user satisfaction. As social media continues to evolve, the role of personalization in shaping the future of content discovery will only become more critical, underscoring the importance of ongoing innovation and refinement in recommender system technologies.

9.4. Case Study 4: Online Advertising

Online advertising represents a crucial domain where recommender systems play a pivotal role in enhancing the relevance and effectiveness of ad placements. This case study delves into the implementation and impact of recommendation algorithms within the context of online advertising, exploring the methodologies employed, the challenges encountered, and the outcomes achieved. By examining the nuances of ad recommendation systems, we can elucidate their critical function in optimizing ad delivery, maximizing user engagement, and driving business revenue.

In the digital advertising ecosystem, the primary objective of ad recommendation systems is to present users with ads that are most relevant to their interests and likely to elicit a positive response. This personalized approach contrasts sharply with traditional, untargeted advertising methods, which often suffer from inefficiencies and low engagement rates. By leveraging data-driven insights, recommender systems enhance the precision of ad targeting, thereby increasing click-through rates (CTR), conversion rates, and overall return on investment (ROI) for advertisers.

The foundation of ad recommendation systems lies in the collection and analysis of extensive user data. This data encompasses explicit feedback, such as clicks on ads, conversions, and purchase history, as well as implicit feedback, such as browsing behavior, search queries, and time spent on web pages. By integrating these diverse data sources, the recommendation system constructs detailed user profiles that capture individual preferences, behaviors, and demographic attributes. For instance, a user who frequently searches for travel-related content and books flights online will have a profile reflecting these interests, guiding the recommendation system to present travel ads.

Collaborative filtering and **content-based filtering** are the primary algorithms employed in ad recommendation systems. Collaborative filtering leverages the behavior of similar users to make recommendations. In user-based collaborative filtering, the system identifies users with similar interaction patterns and recommends ads that these similar users have clicked on. Mathematically, the similarity between users u and v can be computed using cosine similarity:

$$sim(u, v) = \frac{\sum_{i \in I_{uv}} r_{ui} r_{vi}}{\sqrt{\sum_{i \in I_u} r_{ui}^2} \sqrt{\sum_{i \in I_v} r_{vi}^2}}$$

where I_{uv} is the set of ads interacted with by both users, and r_{ui} and r_{vi} are the interaction strengths of users u and v, respectively. Item-based collaborative filtering, on the other hand, recommends ads similar to those the user has previously interacted with, such as suggesting ads for related products or services.

Content-based filtering focuses on the attributes of the ads themselves to make recommendations. This involves analyzing features such as ad text, keywords, product

123

categories, and the presence of multimedia elements. For example, if a user frequently clicks on ads for fitness equipment, the system can recommend other ads featuring similar products or brands. The effectiveness of content-based filtering depends on the richness and granularity of the ad metadata and the system's ability to accurately model user preferences based on these features.

Hybrid recommendation systems combine collaborative and content-based filtering to leverage their respective strengths while mitigating their weaknesses. For example, a hybrid system might use collaborative filtering to generate an initial list of recommended ads and then apply content-based filtering to refine this list, ensuring that the suggestions are highly relevant to the user's specific interests. This integrated approach enhances the robustness and accuracy of the recommendations, providing a more personalized ad delivery experience.

Implementing personalized ad recommendation systems involves addressing challenges such as the cold start problem, data sparsity, and scalability. The cold start problem arises when there is insufficient data about new users or new ads, making it difficult to generate accurate recommendations. This issue can be mitigated by leveraging content-based features and using hybrid methods that do not rely solely on user interaction data. Data sparsity, where the user-ad interaction matrix is predominantly empty, is another common challenge. Techniques such as matrix factorization and imputation methods help address this by uncovering latent factors and filling in missing values.

Scalability is a critical consideration in ad recommendation systems, given the vast number of users and the extensive volume of ads being served. Efficient algorithms and data structures are essential to ensure the system can handle the scale and deliver real-time recommendations. Distributed computing frameworks, parallel processing, and optimization techniques such as Approximate Nearest Neighbors (ANN) search are employed to enhance scalability and performance.

The impact of personalized ad recommendations is profound. Personalized ads drive user engagement by presenting content that aligns with individual preferences, reducing ad fatigue and increasing the likelihood of interaction. This increased engagement translates into higher CTRs, as users are more likely to click on ads that are relevant and interesting to them. Additionally, personalized ad recommendations contribute to higher conversion rates, as users are more inclined to take action on ads that resonate with their needs and interests. For example, presenting ads for fashion products to users who frequently browse clothing websites can lead to increased purchases and improved ROI for advertisers.

Empirical studies and real-world implementations have demonstrated the effectiveness of personalized ad recommendation systems. Companies like Google, Facebook, and Amazon have leveraged these systems to enhance ad targeting and drive significant revenue growth. Google's AdWords, for instance, uses advanced machine learning algorithms to match ads with user search queries and browsing behavior, optimizing ad relevance and performance. Facebook's ad recommendation engine employs collaborative filtering and deep learning techniques to deliver highly personalized ads based on user interactions and social connections. Amazon's recommendation system suggests sponsored products alongside organic search results, enhancing the visibility and attractiveness of the ads.

In conclusion, personalized ad recommendation systems are powerful tools that enhance ad relevance, increase user engagement, and drive business revenue. By leveraging collaborative filtering, content-based filtering, and hybrid approaches, these systems provide tailored ad recommendations that align with individual preferences. The implementation of personalized ad recommendation systems involves addressing challenges such as the cold start problem, data sparsity, and scalability, ensuring that the system can deliver accurate and timely recommendations. The impact of personalized ad recommendations on online advertising platforms is significant, leading to higher CTRs, increased conversion rates, and improved ROI. As the digital advertising landscape continues to evolve, the role of personalization in optimizing ad delivery will only become more critical, underscoring the importance of ongoing innovation and refinement in recommender system technologies.

9.5. Lessons Learned and Best Practices

The implementation of recommender systems across diverse domains such as e-commerce, media and entertainment, social media, and online advertising offers valuable insights and lessons that can guide future developments in this field. By reflecting on these experiences, we can distill a set of best practices that enhance the effectiveness, scalability, and user satisfaction of recommendation algorithms. This section synthesizes the key lessons learned from the case studies presented and outlines best practices for designing and deploying robust recommender systems.

One of the most critical lessons learned is the importance of **data quality and diversity**. The performance of recommender systems is intrinsically linked to the quality of the data they rely on. High-quality data that accurately reflects user behavior and preferences is essential for generating relevant and accurate recommendations. Ensuring data diversity is equally important; diverse datasets that capture a wide range of user interactions and content attributes help mitigate biases and improve the generalizability of the models. This involves not only collecting explicit feedback such as ratings and reviews but also integrating implicit feedback such as click-through rates, browsing history, and dwell time. The inclusion of contextual data, such as time of day, location, and device type, further enriches the dataset, enabling more nuanced and context-aware recommendations.

Feature engineering emerges as a vital practice for enhancing model performance. Crafting meaningful features that capture the essence of user preferences and item attributes can significantly improve the predictive power of recommendation algorithms. For instance, in e-commerce, features such as purchase frequency, product categories, and user demographics provide valuable insights that drive personalized recommendations. In media and entertainment, incorporating features like genre, director, and actor information helps align recommendations with user tastes. Effective feature engineering requires a deep understanding of the domain and the ability to translate domain knowledge into quantitative features that the models can leverage.

Addressing the **cold start problem** is another critical lesson learned. The cold start problem, which arises when there is insufficient data about new users or items, can hinder the accuracy of recommendations. Best practices for mitigating this issue include leveraging content-based features to make initial recommendations, using demographic and contextual information to infer preferences, and employing hybrid models that combine collaborative filtering with content-based approaches. For example, a new user in a streaming service might receive recommendations based on their demographic profile and initial interactions, while a new item might be recommended to users with similar tastes based on its content attributes.

The scalability of recommendation algorithms is a paramount concern, especially for platforms with large user bases and extensive catalogs. Techniques such as **matrix factorization, approximate nearest neighbors (ANN) search, and distributed computing frameworks** are essential for ensuring that the system can handle the scale and deliver real-time recommendations. Matrix factorization techniques like Singular Value Decomposition (SVD) and Alternating Least Squares (ALS) decompose the user-item interaction matrix into latent factors, capturing underlying patterns efficiently. ANN search algorithms approximate the nearest neighbors in high-dimensional spaces, reducing computational complexity while maintaining accuracy. Leveraging distributed computing frameworks such as Apache Spark and Hadoop allows for parallel processing of large datasets, enhancing the scalability and performance of the recommendation system.

Evaluation and monitoring are indispensable practices for ensuring the ongoing effectiveness of recommender systems. Offline evaluation using historical data provides a controlled environment for testing different algorithms and configurations, using metrics such as precision, recall, F1-score, mean squared error (MSE), and normalized discounted cumulative gain (NDCG). Online evaluation through A/B testing, interleaving, and multi-armed bandits captures real-time user feedback, providing direct insights into the system's impact on user behavior and engagement. Continuous monitoring of key performance indicators (KPIs) such as click-through rates, conversion rates, and user retention helps identify areas for improvement and guide iterative refinements.

Another essential best practice is ensuring the **fairness and transparency** of recommender systems. As these systems increasingly influence user experiences and business outcomes, it is crucial to address potential biases and ensure equitable treatment of all user groups. Techniques such as fairness-aware recommendation algorithms and bias detection metrics help identify and mitigate biases in the recommendations. Transparency is also vital, providing users with insights into why certain recommendations are made and allowing them to control their preferences and data usage. This builds trust and enhances the overall user experience.

The integration of **advanced machine learning techniques** such as deep learning, reinforcement learning, and natural language processing (NLP) has been shown to significantly enhance the capabilities of recommender systems. Deep learning models, including neural collaborative filtering and convolutional neural networks (CNNs), capture complex, non-linear relationships between users and items, improving recommendation accuracy. Reinforcement learning frames the recommendation process as a sequential decision-making problem, optimizing for long-term user engagement and satisfaction. NLP techniques enable the analysis of unstructured text data, such as user reviews and social media posts, providing additional insights into user preferences and content attributes.

Cross-domain recommendation is an emerging area that leverages data and insights from multiple domains to enhance recommendation quality. For instance, user preferences from an e-commerce platform can inform recommendations on a streaming service, providing a richer understanding of user interests and behaviors. Implementing cross-domain recommendation requires sophisticated data integration and model adaptation techniques to ensure compatibility and relevance across different contexts.

In conclusion, the lessons learned from implementing recommender systems across various domains highlight the importance of data quality, feature engineering, scalability, evaluation, fairness, transparency, and the integration of advanced techniques. By adhering to these best practices, developers can design and deploy robust recommender systems that deliver accurate, relevant, and personalized recommendations, enhancing user satisfaction and achieving business objectives. As the field continues to evolve, ongoing research and innovation will be essential for addressing new challenges and harnessing emerging opportunities, ensuring that recommender systems remain at the forefront of personalization technologies.

9.6. Conclusion

The detailed examination of case studies and practical applications presented in this book highlights the transformative potential of recommender systems across diverse domains. From e-commerce to media and entertainment, social media, and online advertising, these systems have fundamentally altered the way users interact with digital platforms, driving engagement, enhancing user satisfaction, and generating significant business value. This conclusion synthesizes the key insights from the case studies, emphasizing the practical implications and overarching themes that emerge from the application of recommender systems in real-world scenarios.

One of the most striking findings across the case studies is the ability of recommender systems to personalize user experiences effectively. In e-commerce, personalized product recommendations have been shown to significantly increase conversion rates and average order values. By analyzing user behavior, preferences, and historical interactions, these systems can suggest products that are highly relevant to each individual user, thereby enhancing the shopping experience and boosting sales. For instance, Amazon's recommendation engine, which leverages collaborative filtering, content-based filtering, and hybrid approaches, has been pivotal in driving a substantial portion of the company's revenue.

In the realm of media and entertainment, recommender systems have played a crucial role in content discovery. Platforms like Netflix and Spotify use advanced recommendation algorithms to suggest movies, TV shows, and music that align with users' tastes. These systems analyze a multitude of factors, including viewing and listening history, user ratings, and even time of day, to deliver highly personalized content suggestions. The ability to keep users engaged with relevant content not only enhances user satisfaction but also reduces churn rates, ensuring long-term user retention. For example, Netflix's recommendation system, which employs a combination of collaborative filtering, deep learning, and reinforcement learning, has been instrumental in maintaining its vast subscriber base by continuously adapting to users' evolving preferences.

Social media platforms have also harnessed the power of recommender systems to enhance user engagement and interaction. By suggesting relevant posts, friends, groups, and events, these systems help users discover content and connections that resonate with their interests. Algorithms that analyze user interactions, social connections, and content preferences ensure that users are presented with timely and pertinent recommendations, fostering a more engaging and interactive social experience. Facebook's News Feed algorithm, which utilizes machine learning techniques to prioritize posts, has been particularly effective in keeping users engaged by showing them content that is most likely to be interesting and relevant.

In online advertising, recommender systems have revolutionized ad targeting, making it possible to deliver highly personalized advertisements to users. By leveraging detailed user profiles and interaction data, these systems can predict which ads are most likely to resonate with each user, thereby increasing click-through rates and conversion rates. Google's AdWords and Facebook Ads are prime examples of how sophisticated recommendation algorithms can optimize ad delivery, ensuring that users see ads that are relevant to their interests and needs. The use of machine learning models to analyze user behavior and preferences has significantly improved the efficiency and effectiveness of online advertising campaigns.

Despite the numerous benefits, the case studies also underscore the importance of addressing ethical considerations in the deployment of recommender systems. Issues such as algorithmic bias, privacy, and transparency are critical to ensuring that these systems operate fairly and responsibly. For example, bias in recommendation algorithms can lead to the marginalization of certain user groups or the amplification of existing societal inequalities. To mitigate these risks, it is essential to implement fairness-aware algorithms, conduct regular audits, and ensure transparency in how recommendations are generated. Techniques such as differential privacy and federated learning can enhance user privacy while still enabling the personalization of recommendations.

The scalability and adaptability of recommender systems are also crucial for their success in practical applications. As user bases and data volumes grow, these systems must be able to scale efficiently to handle the increased load. Advanced techniques such as distributed computing, parallel processing, and the use of cloud-based infrastructures enable recommender systems to process large datasets in real-time, ensuring that recommendations remain timely and relevant. Additionally, continuous learning and adaptation mechanisms, such as incremental learning and reinforcement learning, allow these systems to stay current with changing user preferences and behaviors, maintaining their effectiveness over time.

In conclusion, the case studies and practical applications of recommender systems demonstrate their significant impact on enhancing user experiences, driving engagement, and generating business value across various domains. The integration of advanced machine learning techniques, the ability to personalize content and recommendations, and the attention to ethical considerations are all critical components of successful recommender systems. As technology continues to evolve, the ongoing research and development in this field will further refine and expand the capabilities of recommender systems, ensuring that they remain at the forefront of digital innovation. The insights gleaned from these case studies provide a robust framework for understanding the practical implications of recommender systems and highlight the potential for continued advancements in the future.

10. Future Trends and Directions

The field of recommender systems is dynamic and ever-evolving, driven by advancements in technology, changing user expectations, and emerging research. As digital commerce continues to grow, the need for sophisticated, personalized recommendation engines becomes increasingly critical. This chapter explores future trends and directions in recommender systems, discussing emerging technologies, ethical considerations, and potential research avenues. By understanding these trends, developers and researchers can stay ahead of the curve and contribute to the next generation of personalized recommendations.

10.1. Emerging Technologies

The landscape of recommender systems is rapidly evolving, driven by advancements in emerging technologies that promise to enhance their capabilities, accuracy, and scalability. This section delves into some of the most significant technological developments that are shaping the future of recommender systems, offering insights into their mechanisms, potential applications, and implications for both users and businesses. By exploring these emerging technologies, we can understand how they contribute to overcoming current limitations and opening new frontiers in personalization and recommendation.

One of the most transformative technologies in this domain is **deep learning**, particularly its application through neural network architectures such as convolutional neural networks (CNNs), recurrent neural networks (RNNs), and attention mechanisms. Deep learning models have shown remarkable success in capturing complex, non-linear relationships between users and items, thereby improving the accuracy of recommendations. For instance, neural collaborative filtering employs deep neural networks to model user-item interactions, enabling the system to learn high-dimensional representations of users and items. These representations capture intricate patterns and nuances in the data that traditional matrix factorization techniques might overlook. The ability of deep learning models to process and integrate various types of data, including text, images, and audio, further enhances their versatility and effectiveness in generating personalized recommendations.

Reinforcement learning is another emerging technology that is gaining traction in the development of recommender systems. Unlike traditional supervised learning methods that rely on static datasets, reinforcement learning models learn to make decisions through interactions with their environment. This dynamic learning process is particularly suited to recommender systems, where user preferences and behaviors are continually evolving. By framing the recommendation task as a sequential decision-making problem, reinforcement learning algorithms optimize long-term user engagement and satisfaction. For example, a reinforcement learning-based recommender system can learn to balance the trade-off between recommending popular items that maximize immediate rewards and suggesting diverse content that promotes long-term user retention. The use of techniques such as Q-learning and policy gradients allows these systems to adapt and improve over time, responding to changing user preferences and market conditions.

Graph neural networks (GNNs) represent another cutting-edge technology with significant implications for recommender systems. GNNs excel at capturing the relationships and dependencies between entities in a graph structure, making them ideal for modeling user-item interactions in a recommendation context. By representing users and items as nodes in a graph and their interactions as edges, GNNs can learn rich embeddings that encapsulate the collaborative signals within the data. These embeddings can then be used to generate more accurate and contextually relevant recommendations. For example, a GNN-based recommender system can leverage social network data to incorporate the influence of social connections on user preferences, thereby enhancing the personalization and relevance of the recommendations.

The integration of **natural language processing (NLP)** techniques is also revolutionizing the way recommender systems interpret and utilize unstructured text data. NLP technologies enable the analysis of user reviews, social media posts, and other textual content to extract meaningful insights about user preferences and item attributes. Techniques such as sentiment analysis, topic modeling, and word embeddings (e.g., Word2Vec, BERT) allow recommender systems to understand the context and sentiment behind user interactions, thereby improving the accuracy of the recommendations. For instance, by analyzing the sentiment of user reviews, an NLP-enhanced recommender system can identify not only which items are popular but also the specific features that users appreciate or criticize, leading to more nuanced and informed recommendations.

Another emerging technology with significant potential is **federated learning**, which addresses the growing concerns around data privacy and security in recommender systems. Federated learning enables the development of recommendation models across decentralized devices without the need to centralize user data. By training models locally on users' devices and aggregating the results in a privacy-preserving manner, federated learning ensures that sensitive user data remains secure while still benefiting from collaborative learning. This approach is particularly valuable in scenarios where data privacy regulations, such as GDPR, impose strict constraints on data sharing and processing. Federated learning not only enhances user privacy but also allows for real-time personalization, as the models can be updated continuously based on local interactions.

The advent of **quantum computing** presents another frontier for recommender systems, with the potential to revolutionize computational capabilities and

132

optimization techniques. Quantum computing leverages the principles of quantum mechanics to perform complex computations at unprecedented speeds, enabling the processing of vast amounts of data and the solving of optimization problems that are currently infeasible for classical computers. For recommender systems, quantum algorithms such as quantum annealing and variational quantum eigensolvers offer the promise of more efficient and accurate optimization of recommendation models. While the practical implementation of quantum computing in recommender systems is still in its early stages, ongoing research and development are paving the way for future breakthroughs.

The incorporation of **augmented reality (AR) and virtual reality (VR)** into recommender systems is also gaining momentum, particularly in the context of e-commerce and entertainment. AR and VR technologies provide immersive and interactive experiences that can significantly enhance the way users engage with recommendations. For instance, in an e-commerce setting, AR can enable users to visualize products in their real-world environment before making a purchase, while VR can offer virtual tours of destinations or interactive previews of video content. By integrating AR and VR capabilities, recommender systems can provide more engaging and contextually rich recommendations that cater to the evolving expectations of tech-savvy consumers.

In conclusion, the emergence of advanced technologies such as deep learning, reinforcement learning, graph neural networks, natural language processing, federated learning, quantum computing, and augmented and virtual reality is driving the evolution of recommender systems. These technologies offer new capabilities and opportunities to enhance the accuracy, scalability, and personalization of recommendations, addressing existing challenges and opening new frontiers in user experience. As these technologies continue to mature, their integration into recommender systems will further refine and transform the way users discover and interact with content, products, and services. The ongoing research and innovation in this field underscore the dynamic and interdisciplinary nature of recommender systems, highlighting their pivotal role in shaping the future of personalization in the digital age.

10.2. Ethical Considerations

The deployment of recommender systems in various digital platforms has brought significant benefits in terms of personalization, user engagement, and business outcomes. However, the widespread adoption of these systems also raises several ethical considerations that need to be meticulously addressed to ensure that they operate fairly, transparently, and responsibly. This section explores the ethical challenges associated with recommender systems, focusing on issues such as bias, privacy, transparency, and the broader societal implications. By examining these ethical dimensions, we can develop frameworks and practices that guide the responsible use of recommendation technologies.

One of the foremost ethical concerns in recommender systems is **algorithmic bias**. Bias can manifest in various forms, including systemic bias, data bias, and model bias, each potentially leading to unfair and discriminatory outcomes. Systemic bias arises from the broader societal and structural inequalities that are often reflected in the data used to train recommendation algorithms. For example, if a music recommendation system primarily uses data from a demographic that predominantly listens to a specific genre, it may underrepresent other genres, leading to biased recommendations for users from different demographics. Data bias occurs when the training data itself is skewed or unrepresentative, such as when certain user groups or types of interactions are over- or under-represented. Model bias emerges from the assumptions and design choices made during the development of the recommendation algorithm, which may inadvertently favor certain outcomes over others.

To mitigate algorithmic bias, it is crucial to implement fairness-aware algorithms and regular audits of the recommendation system. Techniques such as reweighting, resampling, and adversarial training can be employed to ensure that the model is fair across different user groups. Additionally, fairness metrics such as disparate impact and equal opportunity can be used to measure and monitor the fairness of recommendations. For instance, disparate impact assesses whether the recommendations disproportionately favor or disadvantage specific groups, while equal opportunity ensures that users from different groups have equal chances of receiving relevant recommendations.

Privacy is another critical ethical consideration in recommender systems. The collection and processing of extensive user data necessary for personalized recommendations raise significant privacy concerns. Users often share sensitive information, either explicitly or implicitly, which can be misused if not adequately protected. To address these concerns, it is essential to implement robust data protection measures and adhere to privacy regulations such as the General Data Protection Regulation (GDPR). Techniques such as data anonymization, differential privacy, and federated learning can enhance user privacy. Differential privacy ensures that the inclusion or exclusion of a single user's data does not significantly affect the overall output of the recommendation model, thereby protecting individual privacy. Federated learning enables the training of models across decentralized devices without centralizing user data, ensuring that sensitive information remains on the user's device while still benefiting from collaborative learning.

Transparency in recommender systems is vital for building user trust and ensuring accountability. Users should have a clear understanding of how recommendations are generated and the factors influencing these suggestions. This involves providing explanations for recommendations, enabling users to understand why certain items are suggested and how their data is being used. Techniques such as explainable AI (XAI) can be employed to enhance the transparency of recommendation algorithms. For example, providing feature importance scores or visualizing the contribution of different data points to the final recommendation can help users grasp the underlying mechanisms of the system. Transparency also involves disclosing any commercial or sponsorship influences on recommendations, ensuring that users are aware of potential conflicts of interest.

The **broader societal implications** of recommender systems also warrant careful consideration. These systems have the power to shape user behavior, influence public opinion, and even impact mental health. For instance, social media recommendation algorithms that prioritize sensational or polarizing content to drive engagement can contribute to echo chambers and the spread of misinformation. Similarly, recommendation systems in e-commerce that continuously push high-priced items may encourage consumerism and financial strain. It is essential to balance the goals of maximizing user engagement and business revenue with the ethical responsibility of promoting well-being and informed decision-making.

To address these societal implications, it is important to design recommender systems with a focus on ethical outcomes and societal values. This may involve incorporating public interest criteria into the recommendation algorithms, such as promoting diverse content, encouraging healthy behaviors, and facilitating informed choices. Additionally, involving stakeholders, including users, ethicists, and policymakers, in the design and evaluation of recommender systems can help ensure that these systems align with broader societal goals and values.

Another ethical issue is the **potential for manipulation and exploitation** through recommender systems. By leveraging detailed user profiles and predictive algorithms, there is a risk that these systems can be used to manipulate user behavior in ways that are not in the users' best interests. For instance, a recommendation system designed to maximize ad revenue might prioritize clickbait content that is not genuinely valuable to the user. To prevent such exploitation, it is important to establish ethical guidelines and regulatory frameworks that govern the use of recommender systems, ensuring that they operate in a manner that respects user autonomy and well-being.

In conclusion, the ethical considerations surrounding recommender systems are multifaceted and complex, encompassing issues of bias, privacy, transparency, societal impact, and the potential for manipulation. Addressing these challenges requires a comprehensive approach that integrates fairness-aware algorithms, robust privacy protections, transparent operations, and a commitment to societal values. By adhering to ethical principles and involving diverse stakeholders in the design and evaluation of recommender systems, we can ensure that these technologies are used responsibly and beneficially. The ongoing evolution of recommender systems presents an opportunity to not only enhance user experiences and business outcomes but also to promote fairness, trust, and societal well-being in the digital age.

10.3. Potential Research Avenues

The field of recommender systems is rapidly advancing, driven by the growing demand for personalized experiences across various digital platforms. Despite significant progress, numerous challenges and opportunities remain, presenting fertile ground for future research. This section explores several promising research avenues that have the potential to further enhance the effectiveness, fairness, and applicability of recommender systems. By identifying these areas, we aim to inspire ongoing innovation and contribute to the evolution of this dynamic field.

One of the foremost research avenues is the development of **explainable recommender systems**. As recommender systems become more complex, incorporating advanced machine learning techniques such as deep learning and reinforcement learning, the need for transparency and interpretability grows. Users and stakeholders increasingly demand to understand the rationale behind recommendations, especially in sensitive domains like healthcare, finance, and legal services. Research in this area focuses on creating models that can provide clear, understandable explanations for their recommendations without sacrificing performance. Techniques such as attention mechanisms, interpretable models, and post-hoc explanation methods are being explored to bridge the gap between accuracy and interpretability. For example, attention-based models can highlight the most relevant parts of the input data that influenced the recommendation, providing insights into the decision-making process.

Fairness and bias mitigation continue to be critical areas of research, particularly as recommender systems influence various aspects of users' lives. Ensuring that recommendations are fair and do not systematically disadvantage certain user groups requires the development of new algorithms and evaluation metrics. Research efforts are directed toward creating fairness-aware models that can detect and mitigate biases in the data and the recommendation process. Techniques such as adversarial debiasing, reweighting, and fairness-constrained optimization are being investigated to enhance the equity of recommender systems. Additionally, developing comprehensive fairness metrics that can capture different dimensions of fairness, such as individual fairness and group fairness, is crucial for evaluating and improving these systems.

Context-aware recommendation represents another promising research direction. Traditional recommender systems primarily focus on user-item interactions, often overlooking the contextual factors that influence user preferences and behaviors. Integrating context, such as time, location, weather, and social context, can significantly enhance the relevance and personalization of recommendations. Research in this area explores methods to incorporate contextual information into the recommendation process, leveraging techniques such as context-aware matrix factorization, tensor factorization, and deep learning. For instance, a context-aware recommender system for a music streaming service might suggest different playlists for a user based on the time of day, their location, and their current activity.

The **cold start problem**, which arises when dealing with new users or items with little to no interaction data, remains a significant challenge in recommender systems.

Research efforts are focused on developing hybrid models that combine collaborative filtering with content-based and context-aware approaches to address this issue. Transfer learning and meta-learning are emerging as powerful techniques to tackle the cold start problem by leveraging knowledge from related domains or tasks. For example, a recommender system for a new movie streaming service might use pre-trained models from a related domain, such as book recommendations, to bootstrap the learning process and generate initial recommendations.

Scalability and efficiency are perennial concerns, especially for large-scale recommender systems that need to process vast amounts of data in real-time. Research in this area aims to develop algorithms and data structures that can handle the increasing scale of user interactions and item catalogs. Techniques such as distributed computing, approximate nearest neighbor search, and online learning are being explored to enhance the scalability and efficiency of recommender systems. Additionally, the integration of edge computing and federated learning offers new avenues for processing data closer to the source, reducing latency and improving the responsiveness of recommendations.

Multi-objective optimization in recommender systems is gaining attention as platforms seek to balance various goals, such as maximizing user engagement, ensuring diversity, and promoting fairness. Traditional recommender systems often optimize a single objective, such as accuracy or click-through rate, which can lead to unintended consequences. Research in multi-objective optimization explores methods to balance competing objectives, using techniques such as Pareto optimization, multi-task learning, and reinforcement learning. For instance, a news recommendation system might need to balance the objectives of maximizing user engagement, ensuring diverse viewpoints, and minimizing the spread of misinformation.

The integration of **emerging technologies** such as quantum computing and blockchain also presents intriguing research opportunities. Quantum computing, with its potential to perform complex computations at unprecedented speeds, could revolutionize the optimization and scalability of recommender systems. Research is needed to develop quantum algorithms that can effectively solve the recommendation problem, leveraging quantum principles such as superposition and entanglement. Blockchain technology, on the other hand, offers a decentralized and transparent approach to managing user data and interactions, enhancing privacy and trust in recommender systems. Research efforts are focused on integrating blockchain with recommender systems to create secure and verifiable recommendation processes.

Human-AI collaboration is an emerging research area that explores how recommender systems can augment human decision-making rather than replace it. This involves designing systems that provide recommendations while allowing users to retain control and incorporate their expertise and preferences. Research in this area examines user interfaces, interaction mechanisms, and feedback loops that facilitate effective collaboration between humans and AI. For example, a recommender system for medical decision support might provide treatment recommendations while allowing physicians to adjust parameters and incorporate their clinical judgment.

In conclusion, the field of recommender systems is ripe with research opportunities that promise to enhance their capabilities, fairness, and applicability. From explainable and fairness-aware models to context-aware recommendations, scalability solutions, multi-objective optimization, and the integration of emerging technologies, the potential for innovation is vast. By pursuing these research avenues, we can develop recommender systems that are not only more effective and efficient but also more transparent, fair, and aligned with user and societal values. The ongoing advancements in this field underscore the dynamic and interdisciplinary nature of recommender systems, highlighting their critical role in shaping the future of personalized digital experiences.

10.4. Conclusion

The exploration of future trends and directions in recommender systems highlights the transformative potential of emerging technologies and innovative methodologies. As we conclude this discussion, it is clear that the evolution of recommender systems is set to significantly impact various domains, enhancing personalization and user experience while addressing critical challenges such as bias, scalability, and transparency. This synthesis of future trends not only underscores the importance of ongoing research and development but also provides a roadmap for leveraging these advancements to create more robust, fair, and effective recommendation systems.

The advent of **deep learning** has already begun to redefine the landscape of recommender systems, and its continued integration promises even greater advancements. Deep learning models, with their ability to capture complex, high-dimensional patterns in data, offer unparalleled accuracy in predicting user preferences. Techniques such as convolutional neural networks (CNNs) and recurrent neural networks (RNNs) enable the processing of various data types, including images, text, and sequential data, thus enriching the recommendation process. For instance, CNNs can analyze visual content to recommend similar images or products, while RNNs can model user behavior over time to predict future interactions. As these models become more sophisticated, their ability to provide highly personalized and contextually relevant recommendations will continue to improve.

Another critical trend is the application of **reinforcement learning** in recommender systems. By framing recommendation as a sequential decision-making problem, reinforcement learning optimizes long-term user engagement and satisfaction. This approach allows systems to learn from user interactions in real-time, continuously adapting to changes in user preferences and behavior. Techniques such as Q-learning and policy gradient methods enable the development of recommendation policies that balance short-term rewards, such as immediate clicks or purchases, with long-term goals like user retention and satisfaction. The dynamic nature of reinforcement learning makes it particularly suited to environments where user preferences are constantly evolving, such as social media and e-commerce platforms.

The rise of **graph neural networks (GNNs)** represents another promising direction for future research. GNNs excel at modeling the relationships and dependencies between entities in a graph structure, making them ideal for capturing the complex interactions in recommender systems. By representing users and items as nodes and their interactions as edges, GNNs can learn rich embeddings that encapsulate collaborative signals. These embeddings can then be used to generate more accurate and contextually aware recommendations. For example, a GNN-based recommender system can leverage social network data to incorporate the influence of social connections on user preferences, thereby enhancing the personalization and relevance of recommendations.

Natural language processing (NLP) techniques are also poised to play a significant role in the future of recommender systems. NLP enables the analysis of unstructured text data, such as user reviews, social media posts, and other textual content, providing deeper insights into user preferences and item attributes. Techniques such as sentiment analysis, topic modeling, and advanced language models like BERT (Bidirectional Encoder Representations from Transformers) can be used to understand the context and sentiment behind user interactions. This understanding can enhance the quality of recommendations by aligning them more closely with users' expressed preferences and needs.

Federated learning is an emerging technology that addresses the growing concerns around data privacy and security in recommender systems. Federated learning allows models to be trained across decentralized devices without centralizing user data, thus enhancing privacy. By aggregating locally computed updates rather than raw data, federated learning ensures that sensitive information remains on the user's device. This approach not only protects user privacy but also enables real-time personalization by continuously updating the model based on local interactions. As data privacy regulations become more stringent, federated learning will play a crucial role in the ethical deployment of recommender systems.

The potential of **quantum computing** in recommender systems is another exciting frontier. Quantum computing leverages the principles of quantum mechanics to perform complex computations at unprecedented speeds. Quantum algorithms such as quantum annealing and variational quantum eigensolvers offer the promise of more efficient and accurate optimization of recommendation models. While the practical implementation of quantum computing in recommender systems is still in its early stages, ongoing research is paving the way for future breakthroughs that could revolutionize the scalability and efficiency of these systems.

Ethical considerations remain a paramount concern as recommender systems evolve. Ensuring fairness, transparency, and accountability is crucial for building user trust and promoting equitable outcomes. Bias mitigation techniques, transparency mechanisms, and ethical guidelines are essential for addressing the potential negative impacts of recommender systems. For instance, fairness-aware algorithms and regular audits can help detect and correct biases, while explainable AI techniques can provide users with clear insights into the recommendation process. As recommender systems become more pervasive, adhering to ethical principles will be key to their sustainable and responsible development.

In conclusion, the future of recommender systems is shaped by a confluence of advanced technologies and innovative methodologies that promise to enhance their capabilities and address existing challenges. Deep learning, reinforcement learning, graph neural networks, natural language processing, federated learning, and quantum computing are at the forefront of this evolution, each offering unique advantages and opportunities for improvement. Ethical considerations, including fairness, transparency, and privacy, will continue to guide the responsible deployment of these systems. As research and development progress, the integration of these emerging trends will enable recommender systems to deliver more personalized, accurate, and equitable recommendations, ultimately enhancing user experiences and driving business success in an increasingly digital world.

11. Conclusion

In the rapidly evolving landscape of digital commerce, personalization has emerged as a cornerstone of user engagement and satisfaction. Recommender systems, with their ability to tailor content and product suggestions to individual preferences, have become indispensable tools for businesses seeking to enhance customer experiences and drive growth. This book has aimed to provide a comprehensive understanding of recommender systems, from foundational concepts to advanced techniques, practical applications, and future directions. In this concluding chapter, we reflect on the key insights and lessons learned throughout our journey, emphasizing the importance of continuous learning and adaptation in this dynamic field.

11.1. Recap of Key Concepts

Throughout this comprehensive exploration of recommender systems, we have delved into the foundational principles, advanced methodologies, and emerging trends that define this dynamic field. Recommender systems have become an indispensable part of the digital ecosystem, playing a crucial role in personalizing user experiences across various domains, including e-commerce, media and entertainment, social media, and online advertising. This section provides a thorough recap of the key concepts discussed, highlighting the critical findings and their implications for future developments in recommendation technologies.

At the core of recommender systems lie **collaborative filtering** and **content-based filtering**, two fundamental approaches that have shaped the initial landscape of personalized recommendations. Collaborative filtering relies on the collective behavior of users to make recommendations, leveraging user-item interaction matrices to identify patterns and similarities. This approach can be divided into user-based and item-based collaborative filtering. User-based collaborative filtering identifies users with similar preferences and recommends items that these similar users have liked. Conversely, item-based collaborative filtering recommends items that are similar to those the user has interacted with, based on the interactions of other users. Despite their effectiveness, these methods face challenges such as data sparsity and the cold start problem, necessitating the development of more sophisticated models.

Content-based filtering addresses some of these challenges by focusing on the attributes of items rather than user interactions. This approach recommends items similar to those the user has previously liked, based on a comparison of item features. For example, a content-based recommender for movies might use attributes such as genre, director, and cast to suggest films similar to those a user has rated highly. The

141

effectiveness of content-based filtering depends heavily on the richness and accuracy of the item attributes and the system's ability to model user preferences based on these features.

To overcome the limitations of individual methods, **hybrid recommender systems** have been developed, combining collaborative filtering, content-based filtering, and other techniques to leverage their respective strengths. Hybrid models can take various forms, such as blending the outputs of different recommenders, using one method to refine the results of another, or incorporating additional contextual information to enhance recommendations. These systems provide a more robust and comprehensive approach to personalization, improving accuracy and relevance by addressing the weaknesses of single-method approaches.

A critical challenge for recommender systems is the **cold start problem**, which arises when there is insufficient data about new users or items. Various strategies have been proposed to mitigate this issue, including leveraging content-based features, using demographic information, and employing transfer learning to transfer knowledge from related domains. For instance, a new user on a streaming service might receive initial recommendations based on their demographic profile and early interactions, while a new item might be recommended to users with similar tastes based on its content attributes.

The incorporation of **contextual information** represents a significant advancement in the field of recommender systems. Context-aware recommendations consider factors such as time, location, weather, and user activity, providing more relevant and personalized suggestions. For example, a music streaming service might recommend different playlists based on whether the user is at the gym, commuting, or relaxing at home. Context-aware models utilize techniques such as context-aware matrix factorization and tensor factorization to integrate contextual variables into the recommendation process, enhancing the system's ability to adapt to the user's current situation.

Deep learning has revolutionized recommender systems by enabling the modeling of complex, high-dimensional relationships in the data. Techniques such as convolutional neural networks (CNNs) and recurrent neural networks (RNNs) have been employed to process various data types, including images, text, and sequential data. Neural collaborative filtering, which incorporates deep neural networks, captures intricate patterns in user-item interactions, improving recommendation accuracy. Additionally, attention mechanisms and transformer models have been utilized to focus on the most relevant parts of the input data, further enhancing the interpretability and effectiveness of deep learning-based recommender systems.

Reinforcement learning offers another promising direction, framing the recommendation process as a sequential decision-making problem. By optimizing for long-term user engagement, reinforcement learning algorithms can balance short-term rewards, such as immediate clicks or purchases, with long-term goals like user retention and satisfaction. Techniques such as Q-learning and policy gradients enable recommender systems to learn and adapt from user interactions in real-time, providing a dynamic and responsive recommendation experience.

Addressing **ethical considerations** such as fairness, transparency, and privacy is crucial for the responsible deployment of recommender systems. Algorithmic biases can lead to unfair and discriminatory outcomes, necessitating the development of fairness-aware models and regular audits. Transparency in recommendation processes builds user trust and accountability, with explainable AI techniques providing insights into the decision-making mechanisms. Privacy concerns are addressed through robust data protection measures, including differential privacy and federated learning, ensuring that sensitive user data is handled responsibly and securely.

The potential of **emerging technologies** such as quantum computing and blockchain presents exciting opportunities for further advancements. Quantum computing can revolutionize the optimization and scalability of recommender systems, while blockchain technology offers a decentralized and transparent approach to managing user data and interactions. The integration of these technologies promises to enhance the efficiency, security, and trustworthiness of recommendation processes.

In conclusion, the field of recommender systems is characterized by continuous innovation and evolution. By leveraging a combination of collaborative filtering, content-based filtering, hybrid models, deep learning, reinforcement learning, and context-aware techniques, we can develop recommender systems that are highly personalized, accurate, and adaptable. Addressing ethical considerations and integrating emerging technologies will further enhance the effectiveness and responsible deployment of these systems. As we look to the future, ongoing research and development will be essential for pushing the boundaries of what recommender systems can achieve, ensuring that they remain at the forefront of personalization technologies and continue to deliver significant benefits to users and businesses alike.

11.2. Advanced Techniques and Emerging Trends

The domain of recommender systems is continuously evolving, driven by the integration of advanced techniques and the emergence of new trends that aim to enhance the accuracy, scalability, and personalization of recommendations. This section delves into the sophisticated methodologies and technological innovations that are shaping the future of recommender systems. By examining these advancements, we can gain a deeper understanding of their mechanisms, potential applications, and the implications they hold for the future of personalized recommendations.

One of the most significant advancements in recommender systems is the adoption of **deep learning** techniques. Deep learning models, particularly those utilizing neural network architectures such as convolutional neural networks (CNNs), recurrent neural networks (RNNs), and transformers, have demonstrated exceptional performance in capturing complex, non-linear relationships within data. Neural collaborative filtering, for instance, employs deep neural networks to model user-item interactions, capturing intricate patterns that traditional matrix factorization methods might miss. By learning high-dimensional embeddings for users and items, these models can uncover latent features that drive preferences and behaviors, thereby improving recommendation accuracy. The flexibility of deep learning allows for the integration of various data types, including text, images, and audio, enhancing the system's ability to provide comprehensive and nuanced recommendations.

Reinforcement learning represents another advanced technique gaining prominence in recommender systems. Unlike traditional supervised learning methods, which rely on static datasets, reinforcement learning models learn by interacting with their environment, optimizing actions to maximize cumulative rewards. This approach is particularly well-suited to the dynamic nature of recommendation tasks, where user preferences and behaviors evolve over time. By framing the recommendation process as a sequential decision-making problem, reinforcement learning algorithms can balance immediate rewards, such as clicks or purchases, with long-term objectives like user satisfaction and retention. Techniques such as Q-learning and policy gradient methods enable the development of recommendation policies that adapt in real-time, providing personalized and contextually relevant suggestions. For example, a reinforcement learning-based system might prioritize diverse content to avoid user fatigue while still recommending items with high engagement potential.

The integration of **graph neural networks (GNNs)** into recommender systems is another emerging trend with significant potential. GNNs are particularly effective at capturing the relationships and dependencies between entities in a graph structure, making them ideal for modeling user-item interactions. By representing users and items as nodes and their interactions as edges, GNNs can learn rich embeddings that encapsulate the collaborative signals within the data. These embeddings can then be used to generate more accurate and context-aware recommendations. For instance, a GNN-based recommender system might leverage social network data to incorporate the influence of social connections on user preferences, enhancing the personalization and relevance of recommendations. The ability of GNNs to model complex dependencies and multi-hop relationships offers a powerful tool for capturing the intricate patterns in user behavior.

Natural language processing (NLP) techniques have also made significant contributions to the field of recommender systems. NLP enables the analysis of unstructured text data, such as user reviews, social media posts, and other textual content, providing deeper insights into user preferences and item attributes. Advanced language models like BERT (Bidirectional Encoder Representations from Transformers) and GPT-3 (Generative Pre-trained Transformer 3) can understand context and semantics at a high level, allowing for more accurate sentiment analysis, topic modeling, and text-based recommendations. For example, by analyzing user reviews, an NLP-enhanced recommender system can identify the features that users appreciate or criticize, leading to more informed and nuanced recommendations. The ability to process and understand natural language enhances the system's capability to align recommendations with users' expressed preferences and needs.

Federated learning addresses the growing concerns around data privacy and security in recommender systems. Traditional recommendation models often require centralized data collection, raising significant privacy issues. Federated learning offers a solution by enabling the training of models across decentralized devices without centralizing user data. This approach ensures that sensitive information remains on the user's device, enhancing privacy while still benefiting from collaborative learning. By aggregating locally computed updates rather than raw data, federated learning mitigates privacy risks and allows for continuous model improvement. This technique is particularly valuable in scenarios where data privacy regulations, such as GDPR, impose strict constraints on data sharing and processing.

The potential of **quantum computing** in recommender systems represents a futuristic yet promising avenue of research. Quantum computing leverages the principles of quantum mechanics to perform complex computations at unprecedented speeds. Quantum algorithms, such as quantum annealing and variational quantum eigensolvers, offer the promise of more efficient and accurate optimization of recommendation models. For recommender systems, this could translate into faster processing of large-scale data and more effective handling of optimization tasks. While practical implementation is still in its early stages, ongoing research is paving the way for future breakthroughs that could revolutionize the scalability and efficiency of recommendation algorithms.

Multi-objective optimization is gaining traction as recommender systems aim to balance various goals simultaneously, such as maximizing user engagement, ensuring diversity, and promoting fairness. Traditional systems often optimize a single objective, such as accuracy, which can lead to unintended consequences. Multi-objective optimization techniques, such as Pareto optimization and multi-task learning, allow for the consideration of multiple criteria, ensuring a more holistic approach to recommendation. For instance, a news recommendation system might need to balance the objectives of maximizing user engagement, ensuring diverse viewpoints, and minimizing the spread of misinformation. By optimizing for multiple objectives, recommender systems can better align with both user preferences and ethical considerations.

Ethical considerations remain a critical area of focus in the development of recommender systems. Ensuring fairness, transparency, and accountability is essential for building user trust and promoting equitable outcomes. Bias mitigation techniques, transparency mechanisms, and ethical guidelines are vital for addressing potential negative impacts. For example, fairness-aware algorithms and regular audits can help detect and correct biases, ensuring that recommendations do not systematically disadvantage certain user groups. Transparency in recommendation processes, facilitated by explainable AI techniques, allows users to understand and trust the system's decisions. These ethical considerations are crucial for the responsible deployment of recommender systems and their sustainable integration into society.

In conclusion, the integration of advanced techniques and the emergence of new trends are driving the evolution of recommender systems, enhancing their capabilities and addressing existing challenges. Deep learning, reinforcement learning, graph neural networks, natural language processing, federated learning, and quantum computing are at the forefront of this evolution, each offering unique advantages and opportunities for improvement. Multi-objective optimization and ethical considerations further enhance the effectiveness and responsible deployment of these systems. As research and development continue to progress, these advanced techniques and emerging trends will shape the future of recommender systems, ensuring they remain at the cutting edge of personalization technologies and continue to deliver significant benefits to users and businesses alike.

11.3. Ethical Considerations

As recommender systems become increasingly integral to our digital experiences, the ethical considerations surrounding their development and deployment grow in importance. These systems, designed to personalize content and recommendations based on user data, have far-reaching implications that extend beyond technical performance metrics. They influence user behavior, shape public opinion, and can impact societal norms. Therefore, it is crucial to address the ethical dimensions of recommender systems comprehensively, ensuring that they are designed and implemented in ways that are fair, transparent, and respectful of user privacy.

One of the foremost ethical concerns in recommender systems is **algorithmic bias**. Bias can enter recommender systems at various stages, from data collection to model training and decision-making. Systemic bias reflects societal inequalities present in the data, while model bias stems from the assumptions and algorithms used in building the system. These biases can lead to unfair outcomes, such as the marginalization of certain user groups or the overrepresentation of particular viewpoints. For instance, a music recommender system trained predominantly on Western pop music might underrepresent genres from other cultures, thereby not catering to users with diverse musical tastes. Addressing algorithmic bias requires a multifaceted approach, including the diversification of training data, the use of fairness-aware algorithms, and regular audits to detect and mitigate bias. Techniques such as reweighting, resampling, and adversarial debiasing can help ensure that the recommendations are equitable across different user groups.

Transparency in recommender systems is another critical ethical consideration. Users have the right to understand how recommendations are generated and what factors influence these suggestions. Transparency builds trust and allows users to make informed decisions about their engagement with the system. Explainable AI (XAI) techniques play a vital role in enhancing transparency by providing insights into the decision-making process of recommendation algorithms. For example, feature importance analysis can highlight which user behaviors or item attributes contributed most to a particular recommendation. Visualization tools and user-friendly explanations can further demystify the recommendation process, helping users understand why certain content is suggested to them. Additionally, transparency involves disclosing any commercial or sponsorship influences on recommendations, ensuring that users are aware of potential conflicts of interest.

Privacy concerns are paramount when dealing with the extensive user data required for personalized recommendations. Users often provide sensitive information, either explicitly or implicitly, which can be misused if not adequately protected. Ensuring robust data privacy involves implementing stringent data protection measures and adhering to regulations such as the General Data Protection Regulation (GDPR). Techniques like data anonymization, differential privacy, and federated learning enhance privacy by minimizing the risk of data breaches and unauthorized access. Differential privacy ensures that the inclusion or exclusion of a single user's data does not significantly impact the overall model output, thereby protecting individual privacy. Federated learning allows models to be trained across decentralized devices without centralizing user data, maintaining privacy while still benefiting from collaborative learning.

The broader **societal impact** of recommender systems also warrants careful consideration. These systems can shape user behavior and public opinion, sometimes in unintended and harmful ways. For example, social media recommender algorithms that prioritize sensational or polarizing content to drive engagement can contribute to the spread of misinformation and the formation of echo chambers. This can exacerbate societal divisions and undermine informed public discourse. Similarly, recommender systems in e-commerce that continuously push high-priced items may encourage unsustainable consumer behavior and financial strain. Balancing the goals of maximizing user engagement and business revenue with ethical responsibilities involves designing algorithms that promote diverse, accurate, and beneficial content. Incorporating public interest criteria into recommendation algorithms can help align their outputs with societal values, such as promoting diverse perspectives and encouraging healthy behaviors.

Manipulation and exploitation through recommender systems present another ethical challenge. Detailed user profiles and predictive algorithms can be used to manipulate user behavior for commercial gain, often without the user's knowledge or consent. For instance, a recommendation system designed to maximize ad revenue might prioritize clickbait content that is not genuinely valuable to the user. To prevent such exploitation, it is essential to establish ethical guidelines and regulatory frameworks governing the use of recommender systems. These frameworks should ensure that the systems operate in a manner that respects user autonomy and promotes their well-being. User consent and control over their data and recommendations are critical components of ethical recommender systems.

In conclusion, the ethical considerations surrounding recommender systems are complex and multifaceted, encompassing issues of bias, transparency, privacy, societal impact, and the potential for manipulation. Addressing these challenges requires a comprehensive approach that integrates fairness-aware algorithms, robust privacy protections, transparent operations, and a commitment to societal values. By adhering to ethical principles and involving diverse stakeholders in the design and evaluation of recommender systems, we can ensure that these technologies are used responsibly and beneficially. As recommender systems continue to evolve, their ethical deployment will be crucial for maintaining user trust and promoting equitable outcomes in the digital age. The insights and practices discussed in this section provide a foundation for developing recommender systems that are not only technically proficient but also ethically sound, aligning technological advancement with the broader goals of societal well-being and justice.

11.4. Continuous Learning and Adaptation

In the dynamic landscape of digital interactions, the ability of recommender systems to continuously learn and adapt is crucial for maintaining their relevance and effectiveness. Continuous learning and adaptation refer to the ongoing process by which recommender systems update their models in response to new data and changing user preferences. This section explores the mechanisms and methodologies that enable recommender systems to remain current and responsive, ensuring that they deliver personalized and accurate recommendations over time. By understanding these processes, we can appreciate the sophistication and necessity of adaptive systems in a constantly evolving digital environment.

At the heart of continuous learning and adaptation in recommender systems is the concept of **incremental learning**. Unlike traditional batch learning, where models are trained on a fixed dataset, incremental learning involves updating the model as new data arrives. This approach allows the system to incorporate fresh information and refine its predictions continuously. For example, an e-commerce recommender system can update its recommendations based on real-time user interactions, such as recent purchases or browsing behavior. Incremental learning algorithms, such as online gradient descent and stochastic gradient descent (SGD), are designed to handle streaming data efficiently, enabling the model to adapt quickly without the need for complete retraining.

Reinforcement learning offers another powerful framework for continuous adaptation. In reinforcement learning, the recommender system is treated as an agent that learns by interacting with its environment and receiving feedback in the form of rewards or penalties. This feedback loop allows the system to refine its recommendation policy iteratively, optimizing for long-term user satisfaction and engagement. Techniques such as Q-learning and policy gradient methods enable the system to balance immediate rewards, such as clicks or purchases, with long-term objectives like user retention and loyalty. For instance, a streaming service might use

148

reinforcement learning to recommend a mix of popular and niche content, encouraging users to explore new genres while still enjoying familiar favorites.

Context-aware recommendations represent a significant advancement in adaptive systems. By integrating contextual information such as time of day, location, device type, and user activity, recommender systems can provide more relevant and timely suggestions. Contextual bandit algorithms, which extend the multi-armed bandit problem to include contextual variables, are particularly effective in this regard. These algorithms dynamically adjust the recommendation strategy based on the current context, ensuring that the suggestions are aligned with the user's immediate needs and preferences. For example, a travel app might recommend different activities or destinations depending on whether the user is planning a summer vacation or a winter getaway.

The use of **transfer learning** and **meta-learning** techniques also enhances the adaptability of recommender systems. Transfer learning involves leveraging knowledge from one domain or task to improve performance in another, while meta-learning focuses on learning how to learn more effectively. These approaches are especially useful for addressing the cold start problem, where the system has limited data about new users or items. By transferring knowledge from related domains or learning generalizable features, the system can make informed recommendations even with sparse data. For instance, a new user on a book recommendation platform might receive initial suggestions based on their reading habits from a similar domain, such as movie preferences, leveraging the correlations between the two.

Federated learning is an emerging paradigm that enhances continuous learning while preserving user privacy. In federated learning, models are trained across decentralized devices using local data, and only aggregated updates are shared with the central server. This approach allows the system to continuously learn from distributed data sources without centralizing sensitive information. Federated learning is particularly valuable in contexts where data privacy regulations, such as GDPR, impose strict constraints on data sharing. By enabling continuous and collaborative learning across multiple devices, federated learning ensures that the recommender system remains current and personalized while respecting user privacy.

The integration of **advanced machine learning techniques**, such as deep learning and graph neural networks (GNNs), further amplifies the capacity for continuous adaptation. Deep learning models, including convolutional neural networks (CNNs) and recurrent neural networks (RNNs), can capture complex, non-linear relationships in the data, allowing for more nuanced and accurate recommendations. Graph neural networks, which model the relationships and dependencies between entities in a graph structure, excel at capturing the collaborative signals in user-item interactions. By continuously updating these models with new data, recommender systems can maintain high levels of accuracy and relevance. For example, a social media platform might use a GNN-based recommender system to dynamically adjust friend suggestions and content recommendations based on the evolving social graph.

A/B testing and online evaluation play a crucial role in the continuous improvement of recommender systems. By comparing different versions of the system in real-time, A/B testing allows developers to identify the most effective algorithms and configurations. Online evaluation metrics, such as click-through rate (CTR), conversion rate, and dwell time, provide direct feedback on user engagement and satisfaction. Continuous monitoring of these metrics enables the system to detect and respond to shifts in user behavior, ensuring that the recommendations remain aligned with user preferences. For instance, an online retailer might use A/B testing to evaluate the impact of a new recommendation algorithm on sales and customer retention, iteratively refining the model based on the results.

In conclusion, continuous learning and adaptation are essential for the sustained effectiveness of recommender systems in a dynamic digital environment. By leveraging incremental learning, reinforcement learning, context-aware recommendations, transfer learning, federated learning, and advanced machine learning techniques, these systems can remain responsive and relevant. The integration of A/B testing and online evaluation further supports the continuous improvement of recommendations, ensuring that they meet the evolving needs and preferences of users. As the digital landscape continues to change, the ability of recommender systems to learn and adapt in real-time will be crucial for delivering personalized and engaging user experiences. The advancements discussed in this section highlight the sophistication and necessity of adaptive systems, underscoring their pivotal role in the future of personalized digital interactions.

11.5. Final Thoughts

The journey through the complex and multifaceted world of recommender systems has revealed the profound impact these technologies have on shaping user experiences across a myriad of digital platforms. From the foundational principles of collaborative and content-based filtering to the cutting-edge advancements in deep learning, reinforcement learning, and graph neural networks, recommender systems have continually evolved to meet the growing demand for personalization and relevance. As we conclude this comprehensive exploration, it is essential to reflect on the key insights and their broader implications for the future of recommendation technologies.

The ability of recommender systems to deliver personalized experiences hinges on their capacity to process and analyze vast amounts of user data. This data-driven approach allows these systems to uncover intricate patterns in user behavior and preferences, facilitating the delivery of highly relevant content and product suggestions. However, the reliance on extensive data also brings to the forefront significant ethical considerations, such as privacy, transparency, and fairness. Ensuring that recommender systems operate within ethical boundaries is paramount for maintaining user trust and promoting equitable outcomes. Techniques such as differential privacy, fairness-aware algorithms, and explainable AI provide pathways to address these ethical challenges, ensuring that recommender systems not only perform well but also adhere to societal values.

The continuous learning and adaptation of recommender systems are crucial for their sustained effectiveness in dynamic environments. Incremental learning, reinforcement learning, and context-aware recommendations enable these systems to remain responsive to changing user preferences and behaviors. The integration of advanced machine learning techniques, such as deep learning and graph neural networks, further enhances the ability of recommender systems to capture complex relationships and provide nuanced recommendations. The role of federated learning in preserving user privacy while enabling continuous improvement underscores the importance of innovative approaches in balancing performance with ethical considerations.

The exploration of emerging trends and advanced techniques highlights the potential for further advancements in the field of recommender systems. Quantum computing and blockchain technology present exciting opportunities for enhancing the scalability, efficiency, and security of these systems. Multi-objective optimization and ethical considerations remain at the forefront, guiding the development of recommender systems that balance various goals and promote responsible usage. The potential for human-AI collaboration in recommender systems points to a future where these technologies augment human decision-making, offering personalized insights while respecting user autonomy.

Reflecting on the historical evolution of recommender systems, it is evident that their development has been driven by a combination of theoretical advancements and practical applications. The transition from basic collaborative filtering techniques to sophisticated hybrid models and deep learning approaches illustrates the relentless pursuit of improved accuracy and personalization. Each technological leap has brought with it new challenges and opportunities, underscoring the iterative nature of innovation in this field.

As we look to the future, the ongoing research and development in recommender systems promise to further enhance their capabilities and address existing limitations. The integration of interdisciplinary insights from fields such as psychology, sociology, and human-computer interaction will play a crucial role in designing systems that are not only technically proficient but also user-centric. The ability to understand and model complex user behaviors, incorporate diverse data sources, and provide transparent and fair recommendations will be key to the continued success and acceptance of these systems.

In conclusion, the evolution of recommender systems reflects a broader trend towards personalization and user-centric design in the digital age. These systems have become indispensable tools for navigating the vast amounts of information available online, offering tailored experiences that enhance user satisfaction and engagement. The advancements in machine learning, data processing, and ethical frameworks provide a robust foundation for the future development of recommender systems. As we move forward, the principles and practices discussed in this book will serve as a guide for researchers, developers, and practitioners, ensuring that recommender systems continue to evolve in ways that benefit both users and society at large. The future of recommender systems is bright, promising innovations that will further enrich our digital interactions and experiences.

www.ingramcontent.com/pod-product-compliance
Lightning Source LLC
LaVergne TN
LVHW081528050326
832903LV00025B/1686